DEPARTMENT OF THE ENVIRONMENT, TRANSPORT AND THE REGIONS

Transport Statistics Report

ROAD ACCIDENT STATISTICS ENGLISH REGIONS 1996

Published December 1997

London: The Stationery Office

Prepared for publication by TSA5 branch
Europe, Statistics and Research Directorate
Department of the Environment, Transport and the Regions

Linden Francis

GOVERNMENT STATISTICAL SERVICE

A service of statistical information and advice is provided to the government by specialist staff employed in the statistics divisions of individual Departments. Statistics are made generally available through their publications and further information and advice on them can be obtained from the Departments concerned.

Enquiries about the contents of this publication should be made to:

Europe, Statistics and Research Directorate
Department of the Environment, Transport and the Regions
Zone 1/28
Great Minster House
76 Marsham Street
London SW1P 4DR

Telephone 0171 271 3830
Facsimile   0171 271 3775

Data Service

Copies of the main tables in this publication can be supplied on a computer diskette by the Department of the Environment, Transport and the Regions (at a cost of £60). Further tabulations of road accident statistics are also available from the Department, subject to confidentiality rules. The charges vary with the complexity of the analysis (minimum £60 per data run) and the availability of these services depends upon the resources within the Department. Enquiries should be addressed in writing to Mr L Francis of the Europe, Statistics and Research Directorate at the above address.

Acknowledgements

The Department of the Environment, Transport and the Regions would like to acknowledge the assistance provided by the Police Accident Investigation Unit at Catford.

Contents

Symbols and Conventions

Rounding of Figures:

In tables where figures have been rounded there may be an apparent slight discrepancy between the sum of the constituent items and the independently rounded total.

Symbols:

.. = not available

Conversion Factor:

1 kilometre = 0.6214 mile

Preface

This edition of Road Accident Statistics English Regions (RASER) sets out road accident statistics on a local basis for England, together with national summaries for England, Scotland and Wales. The local dimension set out in this publication supplements the more detailed analysis of road accident statistics published in "Road Accidents Great Britain 1996 - The Casualty Report" (RAGB) in August 1997.

For many years, statistics in RASER have been mostly organised upon a county basis to satisfy two key requirements. These are:

- to show the local distribution of road accident statistics between local highway authorities responsible for highway maintenance and road safety,

- to present a concise account for Great Britain of the local collection of road accident statistics whether collected and processed by local authorities or local police forces.

The former requirement is guided by the need to compare and monitor variations in the nature of road accidents between local areas to highlight the need for intervention at a local level. The analysis of road accidents on different types of road and junction in this publication is a good example. The latter requirement provides a mechanism for monitoring casualty and accident totals in local reporting areas, which is essential for monitoring local progress in target reduction achievement. The analysis of casualty changes in each county by severity group since the 1981 - 85 baseline average is a good example. In particular this type of analysis can provide a broad early warning of untypical changes, which may indicate the effect locally of changes in the understanding of the national reporting requirement, the reporting rate, or changes in the reporting form.

Since 1 April 1996, local authority reorganisation and the creation of more locally focused unitary authorites has meant that the county analysis of road accident statistics does not provide information to satisfy the requirements specified above for the following local areas, although in every case the former local authority fully includes newly established unitary authorities:-

Former County Authority	New Authority (from 1 April 1996)	Casualties 1996 (Calendar Year)
North Yorkshire	North Yorks County	4,105
	York	618
Humberside	Kingston-upon -Hull	1,442
	East Riding of Yorkshire	1,657
	North Lincolnshire	968
	North East Lincolnshire	812
Cleveland	Hartlepool	425
	Redcar and Cleveland	511
	Middlesborough	793
	Stockton-on-Tees	807
Avon	Bristol	1,651
	North Somerset	729
	Bath and North East Somerset	420
	South Gloucestershire	869

On 1 April 1997 the following additional unitary authorities were established:-

Former County Authority	New Authority (from 1 April 1997)
Bedfordshire	Bedfordshire County Luton
Buckinghamshire	Buckinghamshire County Milton Keynes
Derbyshire	Derbyshire County City of Derby
Dorset	Dorset County Poole Bournemouth
Durham	Durham County Darlington
East Sussex	East Sussex County Brighton and Hove
Hampshire	Hampshire County Portsmouth Southampton
Leicestershire	Leicestershire County City of Leicester Rutland
Staffordshire	Staffordshire County Stoke-on-Trent
Wiltshire	Wiltshire County Swindon

In the light of these local organisational changes, the established presentation in RASER will become increasingly out of step with local road safety responsibilities and reporting organisations, and the next publication will be reviewed to accommodate these changes.

The current system of collecting road accident statistics was set up in 1968, and is for the benefit and use of local authorities, the police and central government. Each year, about 235,000 STATS19 road accident report forms (an example of which can be found on pages 56 to 58) are completed by police officers of the 51 police forces in Great Britain. These forms record data about accidents on the public highway which involved personal injury or death. These data are transferred onto magnetic tape or computer diskette and are sent to DETR where they are incorporated into an annual data file.

The principal purpose in collecting and publishing statistics of road accidents is to provide background information for both central government and local authorities about the roads, road users, locations, times of day, weather conditions, etc involved in road accidents. The statistics are used both to guide and monitor policy development, at local and national level, and they provide a source for assessing the effectiveness of remedial measures.

The report also includes data from Northern Ireland. These data, where available, are included with each table along with data for Scotland and Wales. *More detailed statistics for Scotland and Wales are available from the Scottish and Welsh Offices - please refer to the inside rear cover for more details.*

Several of the tables contain averages of 1981-85 data. These represent the base figures which the Secretary of State for Transport used to set the target for reducing the number of road casualties by one third by the year 2000. **It should also be noted that main Tables 1 and 6 which give casualty totals by severity for the years covering 1981 to 1985 have been extended to show revised estimates for London for this period.** At the beginning of September 1984 the Metropolitan police implemented improved procedures for allocating the level of severity to accidents and casualties. The change is thought to have had no effect on overall casualty numbers, but in the period between 1981 and the date of the change it is estimated that there were 4,725 casualties whose injuries were originally judged to be slight but would have been judged serious under the later procedures. However, this is an overall estimate and it is not possible to present similar revised estimates of accidents by road type and other detailed characteristics.

DETR is generally prepared to sell tabulations of road accident data. The cost of data varies with the complexity of each request, but averages about £60 per data run. Further information can be obtained from: - *Mr Linden Francis, Department of the Environment, Transport and the Regions, 1st Floor, Great Minster House, 76 Marsham Street, London, SW1P 4DR, Telephone 0171-271-3830.*

1. Commentary on tables and charts

Linden Francis, Europe, Statistics and Research Directorate , Department of Environment, Transport and the Regions

Introduction

This section gives a review of the tables and charts included in this report. As noted in the preface, and with the exception of table 15, the data are disaggregated either by county, Government Office (GO) region, or Highways Agency (HA) region. Certain tables show United Kingdom (UK)totals where Northern Ireland data is available, UK totals are not shown on tables where Northern Ireland data is unavailable, the relevant tables are annotated accordingly.

From April 1994, the DETR regional offices were subsumed within the Government Offices for regions (GORs). This edition of RASER uses the GORs as the basis for its regional breakdowns (this was first instituted in last year's edition). In order to provide consistent time series, wherever data for earlier years are shown in the tables, these are also on the basis of the new GOR definition. *Note, however, that the regional figures given in this edition will not be consistent with those published in earlier editions. A map showing the GORs can be found on page 51.*

This publication follows Government Statistical Service advice in showing data for the Merseyside GOR both separately and combined with the neighbouring North West GOR. However the Merseyside GOR is much smaller in terms of area, population and traffic than other Government Office regions, therefore it is often not appropriate to make direct comparisons with these other regions. This article refers to the Merseyside GOR when commenting on rates, proportions and extreme cases, but not when discussing absolute numbers of accidents or casualties.

The Highways Agency is responsible for the construction and management of motorways and trunk roads in England. Until April 1994, the management function was carried out by nine Network Management Divisions, covering the same areas as the Department's old Regional Offices. However during 1994, the Agency reduced the number of Network Management Divisions to four, covering wider areas. A separate Annex was added to the 1995 edition of RASER to show these changes and is again included. Each table from the main body of the report which contains GOR data is repeated in Annex A, showing the equivalent figures for the Highways Agency Network Management Division Regions instead. Unless the table headings state otherwise, these tables show data for all road accidents in these regions, not just those occurring on roads for which the Highways Agency is responsible. A map showing the Highways Agency regions can be found on page 53.

It should also be noted that population figures used in this report are final mid-1996 estimates.

Casualties

Table 1 gives the regional distribution of casualties and is presented as a time series for the period 1989 to 1996, together with the average for the years 1981-1985. There has been little significant change in the aggregate casualty distribution between the regions over this period. In each year shown upto and including 1995, London had the highest number of casualties, but in 1996 South East Region overtook London and now has highest number of casualties. Excluding Merseyside from the comparison of casualty levels, the lowest number of casualties was in the North East, which with the exceptions of East Midlands and South West had total casualties less than half of any other region.

The table also shows that in 1996 Merseyside had the highest overall casualty rate per 100,000 population, followed by London and the North West region. The lowest rates were found in the North East and South West regions. London, however, had the lowest fatality rate of all the regions - probably because accidents in urban areas tend to be less severe because they occur at lower speeds. The highest fatality rate was in the East Midlands region with the next highest in the South West and Eastern regions.

Chart 1a depicts the number of casualties killed and the number seriously injured in each region in 1996. The chart shows that the South East, North West/Merseyside regions had the highest number of those killed and London and the South East region the highest number of those seriously injured.

Chart 1b depicts the number of casualties killed or seriously injured (KSI) and slightly injured in each region in 1996 and shows that London had the highest number of killed or seriously injured casualties, South East region had the highest slightly injured casualty figure and North East had the lowest total in both.

Chart 2 depicts the number of child casualties per 100,000 child population in each region in 1996 and shows that North West had the highest rate of children killed or seriously injured and the South West and South East regions the lowest rate. Merseyside had the highest overall rate of child casualties.

Chart 3 shows the number of adult casualties per 100,000 adult population in each region in 1996 and shows that the East Midlands and Eastern regions had the highest rate of adults killed or seriously injured and Merseyside the lowest rate. Merseyside however, had the highest overall rate of adult casualties.

Charts 4 and **5** depict the percentage change in overall casualties and those killed or seriously injured for each region between 1995 and 1996 (the charts take account of the change in regional definition as noted in the introduction). **Chart 4** shows that overall casualties have increased in all of the 11 English regions. **Chart 5** shows that casualties killed or seriously injured fell in five of these regions. Both South West and the Yorkshire/Humberside regions recorded decreases in excess of five per cent. There was an increase of about five per cent in London region.

Local authority casualty comparisons

Tables 2-5 give information on the number of casualties, rate per 100,000 population, and percentage distribution, by age and road user type for each English county, Scotland and Wales.

Table 2 gives the number of casualties by age and road user type for 1996 and **Table 3** gives the same information as an average for the years 1981-1985.

Table 4 gives casualty rates, per 100,000 population, by age and by type of road user for each English county. In England in 1996, 374 children were killed or injured in road accidents per 100,000 children and the county casualty rates varied from 266 in Avon to 503 in Merseyside. The casualty rate for those aged 60 and over varied from 203 in Avon and Cleveland to 345 in North Yorkshire. The overall casualty rate for all ages was lowest in Suffolk and highest in Surrey. The pedestrian casualty rate was highest in most urbanised areas, in particular London and Greater Manchester, and lowest in rural counties such as Oxfordshire, Somerset and Suffolk. The pedal cyclist casualty rate was highest in Cambridgeshire and lowest in Durham. The car occupant casualty rate varied from 244 in Avon to 513 in Surrey.

Table 5 gives the distribution of casualties, by age and by type of road user, for each county. In England in 1996, 14 per cent of road accident casualties were children and 10 per cent were aged 60 and over. The proportion of casualties who were children varied from 9 per cent in Surrey to 21 per cent in Cleveland. Somerset, East Sussex and Dorset had the highest proportion of casualties aged 60 or over; 14 per cent compared with 10 per cent in the whole of England.

Table 6 gives the number of casualties killed or seriously injured and total casualties in each English county for 1996 and compares them with the average for the years 1981-1985. The percentage change is also given. In England as a whole, the number killed or seriously injured has fallen by 38 per cent and overall casualties risen by 1.2 per cent. The number of casualties killed or seriously injured has fallen in every county except Cheshire, with the largest fall, at 71 per cent, recorded in Berkshire. The large variation in the change in total casualties since the baseline between counties will reflect the effects of any changes to reporting procedures during this period.

Casualties by road type

Charts 6a and **6b** depict the number of casualties killed or seriously injured and slightly injured in each region on built-up and non built-up roads respectively. On built-up roads, the highest number of casualties for both severity groups was in London, with the North East having the lowest number for both severity groups. On non built-up roads, the highest number of casualties both killed or seriously injured and slightly injured were in the South East region. East Midlands and the Eastern region also had high numbers of casualties killed or seriously injured. The lowest number of casualties for both severity groups was in London.

Table 7 gives the total number of casualties in each region disaggregated by severity and by road type. In most regions well over 50% of casualties were in accidents on built-up roads. In London the figure was 96%, whereas in the Eastern and South West regions, the figure was only 55%. The North West and South East regions had the highest proportion of casualties on motorways, with 6%. Of the other regions only the West Midlands NW/Merseyside and the

Eastern region had greater than 5% of their casualties on motorways. The proportion of casualties who were killed or seriously injured was highest on non built-up roads. The highest proportion was in the East Midlands region, where 23% of casualties were killed or seriously injured. The East Midlands and London had the highest proportion of KSI to all casualties on built-up roads.

Charts 7 and **8** show, for built-up and non built-up roads respectively, overall casualty numbers on trunk, principal and other roads in each region in 1996. On built-up roads, the highest number of casualties on trunk and principal roads was in London. The NW/Merseyside also had a large number of casualties on other roads. London had four times as many Built up trunk road casualties than the next highest region, which was NW/Merseyside. On non built-up roads the highest number of casualties on trunk roads was in the Eastern region. The highest number of casualties on principal and other roads was in the South East region.

Table 8 gives the casualty rates by severity for motorways and A roads for each region. The casualty rate is derived by dividing the number of casualties on a particular road type by the traffic carried on those roads. The rates are given as an average for the period 1994 to 1996. The highest rate for total casualties on motorways, was in London with the lowest rate being in the South West. The fatality rate on motorways deviated only slightly between the majority of the regions, however the highest was in the North East. London and Merseyside had the highest rate for total casualties on all A roads, with the South West having the lowest rate. For England as a whole, the highest total casualties rate was on built-up trunk and principal roads, and the lowest on motorways.

Accidents

Table 9 gives accident rates by severity for motorways and A roads for each region. The accident rate is derived by dividing the number of accidents on particular road types by the traffic carried on that road type. The rates are given as an average for the period 1994 to 1996. In England over the three year period, built-up principal A roads had the highest all severities accident rate at 101 accidents per 100 million vehicle kilometres. Motorways had the lowest rate, at 11 accidents per 100 million vehicle kilometres. For fatal accidents, the respective rates for these two road types were 1.0 accidents and 0.2 accidents. The highest fatal accident rate is on non-built up principal roads at 1.2 accidents per 100 million vehicle kilometres.

Chart 9 depicts the number of accidents on motorways and trunk and principal A roads in each region in 1996. The South East and NW/Merseyside regions, had the highest number of accidents on motorways, whilst London had the highest number of accidents on trunk and principal A roads.

Seasonal pattern of accidents

The seasonal pattern of injury accidents is given in **Table 10**. The base has been calculated as the average number of accidents per day in each region. The peak months for accidents can vary from year to year for various reasons, for example, differing weather conditions. In 1996 the general pattern is low accident rates in the early part of the year generally building to a peak between the months of September to November. Some regions however had accident rates which rose as early as June and July. The pattern within the two metropolitan regions of London and Merseyside fluctuated greatly and did not reflect the general trend across England. The peak month in 1996 for the all severity accident rate was either October or November for all of the regions. For the fatal or serious accident rate, the same was true with the exception of Merseyside and South West regions which peaked in April and September respectively. The lowest all severity accident rate occurred during either January or March for all regions with the exception of London. The lowest fatal and serious accident rate varied a great deal, however with the exception of two regions (Merseyside and South West), it occurred in the first half of the year.

Accidents by road type

Tables 11-13 show the number of junction and non-junction injury accidents occurring on motorways and trunk and principal A roads. On all motorways in England, 16 per cent of accidents occurred at junctions and roundabouts this figure was 59 per cent on all trunk A roads and 69 per cent on all principal A roads.

Accidents at junctions and roundabouts accounted for about 50% of all trunk A road accidents in most regions. For the North West and West Midlands regions, the corresponding figure was around 64% and 69% for London. For principal A roads, the proportion of accidents at junctions and roundabouts was higher than for trunk roads. For all regions with the exceptions of London, North West, NW/Merseyside and South West the figure was between 60 and 70%. 73% of accidents occurred at junctions/roundabouts in the North west and NW/Merseyside with 77% in London. The South West region had the lowest proportion with 59%.

The proportion of fatal or serious accidents on junctions and at roundabouts was around ten per cent less than the all severities proportion except Eastern regions for trunk A and London for both trunk and principal A roads, where there was little difference between the respective accident severities.

Table 14 gives the total number of injury accidents disaggregated by severity on different types of road in each region and county for 1995 and 1996. The average for the years 1981 to 1985 is also given. The road classifications used are motorways, trunk and principal A roads and all roads.

Table 15 shows injury accidents and casualties by severity, and the vehicles involved, for individual English motorways, including A(M) roads. Eighty four per cent of the vehicles involved were cars or vans while 13 per cent were heavy lorries. Motorways with the highest numbers of accidents per kilometre in 1996 were the M25 (5.2 accidents) and the M63 (4.4 accidents).

Table 16 gives the percentage of accidents on the various types of road within each region. This table should be considered in conjunction with Table 19 which shows the distribution of motor traffic within each region.

Background data

Table 17 gives regional background information on road lengths, home population, area, and licensed vehicle numbers. **Table 18** gives the 1994-1996 average distribution between regions of motor traffic on major roads, and **Table 19** shows the distribution of motor traffic within each region. All road lengths shown in Tables 15 and 17 are taken from the Transport Statistics Report *"Road Lengths in Great Britain 1996"*.

List of charts and tables

CHARTS

Chart 1a: Fatal and serious casualties: by region 1996

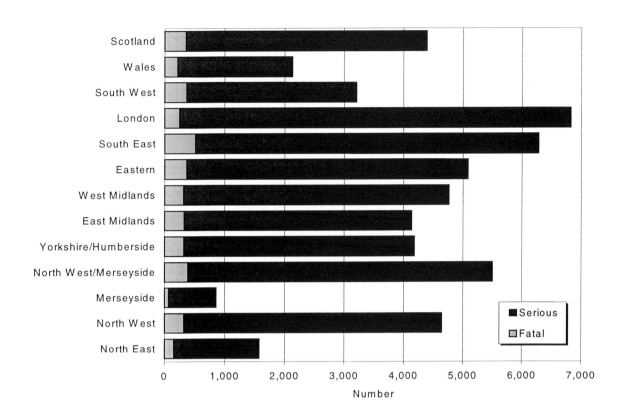

Chart 1b: KSI and slight casualties: by region: 1996

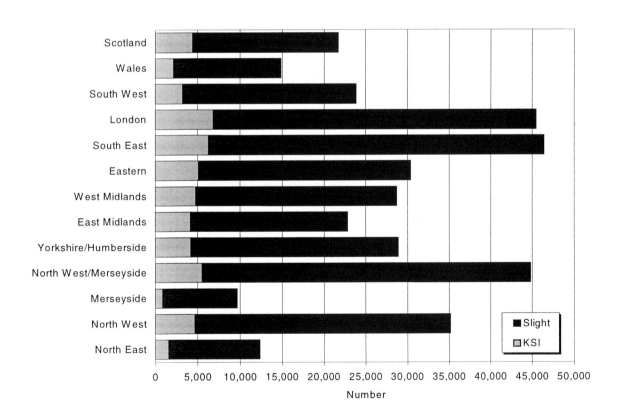

14

Chart 2: Child casualties per 100,000 child population: by severity and region: 1996

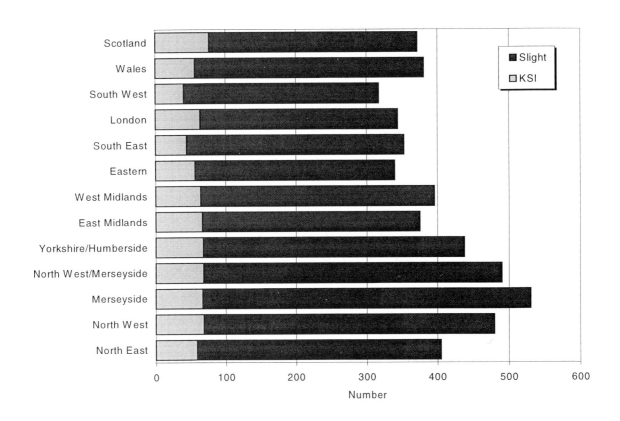

Chart 3: Adult casualties per 100,000 adult population: by severity and region: 1996

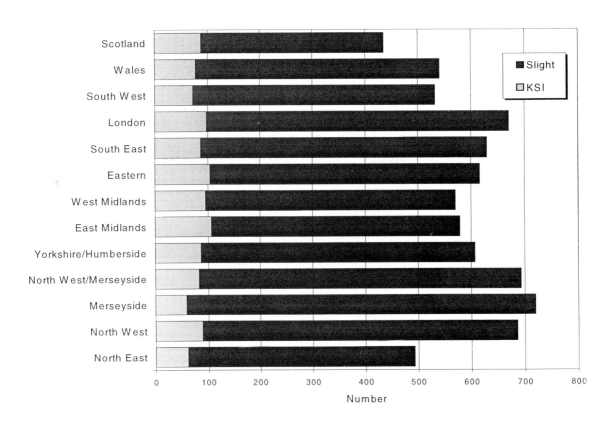

Chart 4: Percentage change in total casualties: by region: 1995-1996

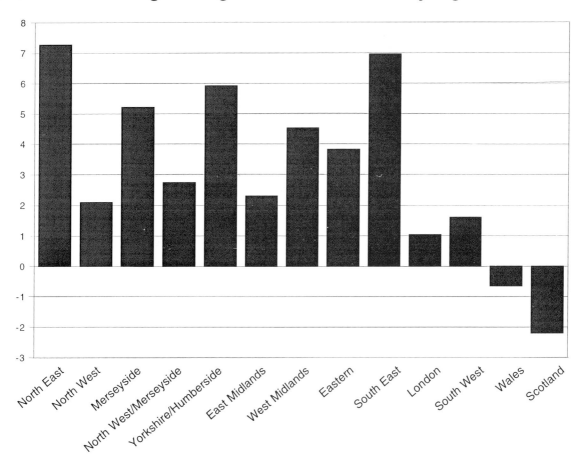

Chart 5: Percentage change in KSI casualties: by region: 1995-1996

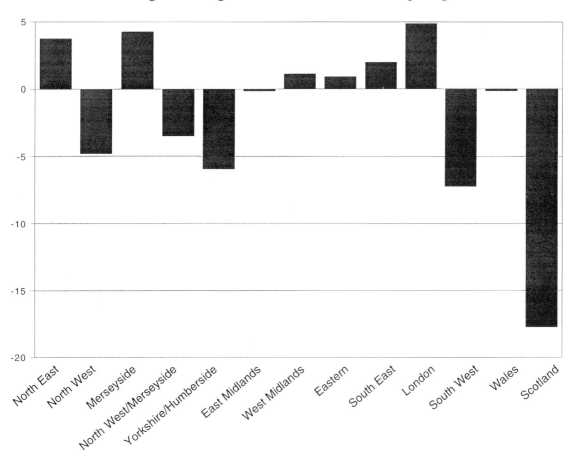

Chart 6a: Casualties on built-up roads: by severity and region: 1996

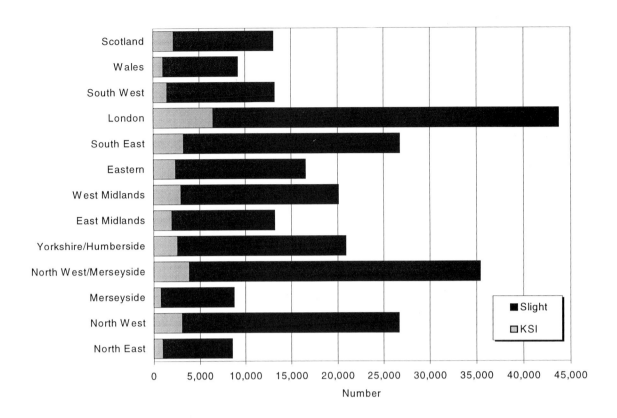

Chart 6b: Casualties on non built-up roads: by severity and region: 1996

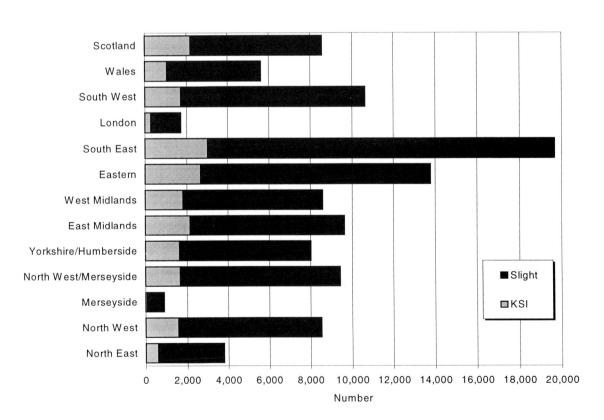

Chart 7: Casualties by road class and region: built-up roads: 1996

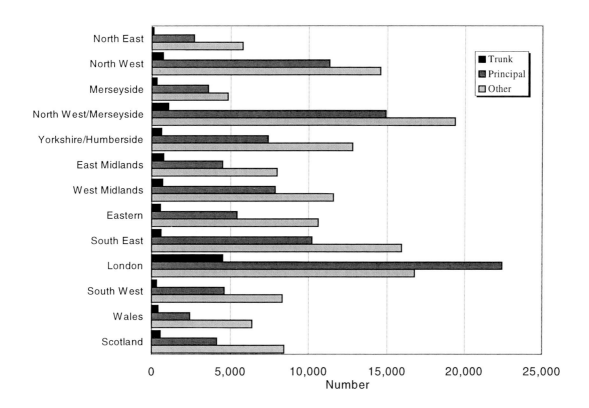

Chart 8: Casualties by road class and region: non built-up roads: 1996

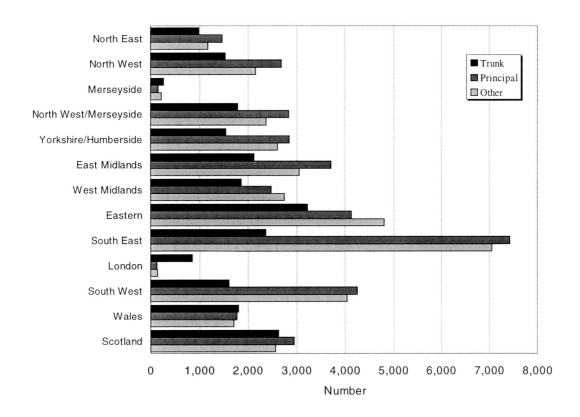

Chart 9: Accidents by road class and region: 1996

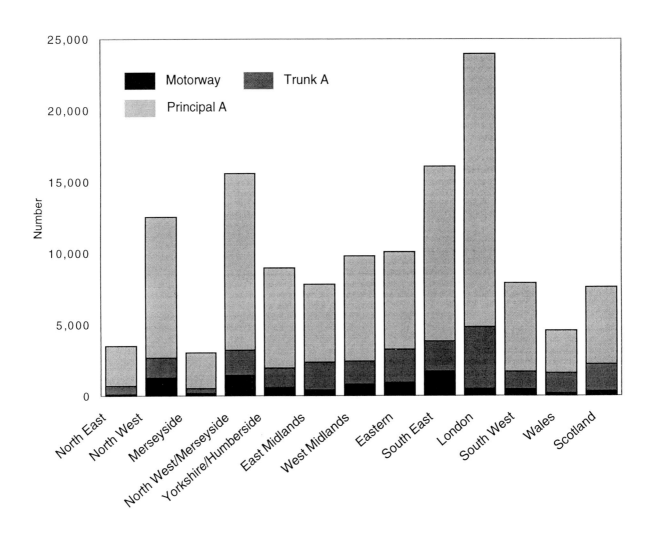

TABLES

1 Casualties: by Government Office Region and severity: 1981-85 average, 1989-1996: rate per 100,000 population, 1996

		1981-85 Average	1989	1990	1991	1992	1993	1994	1995	1996	Rate per 100,000 Population[1]
North East	Fatal	221	210	246	212	161	169	132	152	157	6.0
	KSI	2,637	2,248	2,271	2,043	1,910	1,690	1,673	1,516	1,573	60.5
	Total	11,107	12,741	13,001	12,241	11,935	11,262	11,491	11,514	12,351	474.9
North West	Fatal	486	475	494	449	424	369	350	358	323	5.9
	KSI	5,810	4,993	5,155	4,452	4,306	4,195	4,892	4,875	4,641	84.8
	Total	29,058	33,142	34,238	31,805	32,837	32,691	35,085	34,447	35,166	642.8
Merseyside	Fatal	114	97	81	94	77	71	76	60	66	4.6
	KSI	1,237	1,055	1,094	1,128	1,070	998	923	823	858	60.4
	Total	7,225	8,917	9,511	9,816	10,141	10,437	10,151	9,173	9,651	679.4
North West/Merseyside	Fatal	600	572	575	543	501	440	426	418	389	5.6
	KSI	7,047	6,048	6,249	5,580	5,376	5,193	5,815	5,698	5,499	79.8
	Total	36,284	42,059	43,749	41,621	42,978	43,128	45,236	43,620	44,817	650.3
Yorkshire/Humberside	Fatal	501	480	428	413	414	387	325	345	324	6.4
	KSI	6,830	6,127	5,978	5,202	5,110	4,603	4,357	4,444	4,180	83.0
	Total	25,915	28,560	28,455	26,086	26,599	26,031	27,310	27,279	28,892	573.8
East Midlands	Fatal	492	514	513	410	393	350	341	378	329	7.9
	KSI	6,389	5,342	5,045	4,173	4,145	3,940	3,905	4,140	4,134	99.8
	Total	23,079	25,129	24,852	22,397	22,175	22,207	22,375	22,331	22,845	551.6
West Midlands	Fatal	525	498	478	386	395	353	382	286	319	6.0
	KSI	7,854	6,190	6,136	5,298	4,913	4,514	5,303	4,713	4,765	89.6
	Total	27,691	28,964	30,219	27,425	27,089	26,599	28,114	27,473	28,717	540.1
Eastern	Fatal	533	556	544	493	425	402	391	374	370	7.0
	KSI	8,281	7,318	7,026	5,846	5,648	5,242	5,242	5,040	5,085	96.1
	Total	30,288	35,442	33,973	30,119	29,537	29,510	29,749	29,253	30,370	573.8
South East	Fatal	802	776	762	569	559	531	474	470	517	6.5
	KSI	12,069	9,415	8,769	6,829	6,809	6,273	6,305	6,160	6,283	79.6
	Total	45,503	47,032	46,198	41,860	42,727	41,895	43,976	43,408	46,428	588.0
London	Fatal	539	460	409	368	316	286	270	214	251	3.5
	KSI	8,230	9,344	8,923	7,878	7,233	6,419	6,195	6,510	6,826	96.5
	Total	54,156	52,779	51,995	46,578	46,417	45,927	45,837	44,995	45,457	642.6
South West	Fatal	484	521	468	460	385	310	336	358	368	7.6
	KSI	8,047	5,781	5,424	4,555	4,153	3,916	3,608	3,455	3,206	66.2
	Total	26,352	25,246	25,034	22,515	22,302	22,728	23,413	23,500	23,876	493.2
England	Fatal	4,698	4,587	4,423	3,854	3,549	3,228	3,077	2,995	3,024	6.2
	KSI	67,388	57,813	55,821	47,404	45,297	41,790	42,403	41,676	41,551	84.6
	Total	280,382	297,952	297,476	270,842	271,759	269,287	277,501	273,373	283,753	578.0
Wales	Fatal	259	233	249	227	220	187	210	218	216	7.4
	KSI	3,855	3,191	3,037	2,638	2,537	2,189	2,208	2,133	2,130	72.9
	Total	14,395	16,165	16,432	15,074	14,732	14,331	15,105	14,950	14,853	508.5
Scotland	Fatal	641	553	545	487	460	399	363	408	358	7.0
	KSI	8,887	7,527	6,800	6,131	5,640	4,844	5,570	5,335	4,390	85.6
	Total	27,134	27,475	27,233	25,353	24,182	22,402	22,583	22,183	21,696	423.1
Great Britain	Fatal	5,598	5,373	5,217	4,568	4,229	3,814	3,650	3,621	3,598	6.3
	KSI	80,130	68,531	65,658	56,173	53,474	48,823	50,181	49,144	48,071	84.1
	Total	321,912	341,592	341,141	311,269	310,673	306,020	315,189	310,506	320,302	560.6
Northern Ireland	Fatal	196	181	185	185	150	143	157	144	142	8.5
	KSI	2,362	2,195	2,178	1,833	1,991	1,725	1,805	1,676	1,741	104.7
	Total	8,204	11,611	11,761	10,314	11,264	11,100	12,094	11,725	12,575	756.0
United Kingdom	Fatal	5,794	5,554	5,402	4,753	4,379	3,957	3,807	3,765	3,740	6.4
	KSI	82,492	70,726	67,836	58,006	55,465	50,548	51,986	50,820	49,812	84.7
	Total	330,116	353,203	352,902	321,583	321,937	317,120	327,283	322,231	332,877	566.1

1 Based on 1996 population estimates.

2 Number of casualties: by county and road user type: 1996

	Children (0-15)	Adults (16-59)	Elderly (60+)	All[1] casualties	Pedest-rians	Pedal cyclists	Motor cyclists	Car occupants	Other[2] road users
Avon	507	2,787	368	3,669	563	345	297	2,295	169
Bedfordshire	425	2,398	246	3,069	404	215	214	2,031	205
Berkshire	480	3,170	280	4,124	399	362	343	2,846	174
Buckinghamshire	486	3,143	318	4,110	317	241	260	3,077	215
Cambridgeshire	466	3,721	411	4,692	313	641	315	3,160	263
Cheshire	898	5,317	635	6,850	615	464	370	4,926	475
Cleveland	518	1,822	192	2,536	539	201	62	1,556	178
Cornwall	361	2,110	338	2,809	287	169	268	1,933	152
Cumbria	356	2,005	315	2,676	306	185	204	1,818	163
Derbyshire	672	3,810	479	5,139	582	382	390	3,431	354
Devon	712	3,939	620	5,300	702	371	490	3,435	302
Dorset	415	2,952	537	3,904	374	306	317	2,703	204
Durham	492	2,289	283	3,064	440	169	119	2,079	257
East Sussex	573	3,246	634	4,453	667	299	338	2,860	289
Essex	1,056	6,667	857	8,997	918	686	703	6,132	558
Gloucestershire	284	1,927	311	2,522	284	191	226	1,644	177
Greater London	5,012	33,874	3,814	45,457	9,169	4,309	5,886	22,654	3,439
Greater Manchester	2,753	12,399	1,320	16,472	2,914	1,235	511	10,692	1,120
Hampshire	1,200	7,316	1,018	9,534	1,004	1,034	851	6,098	547
Hereford & Worcester	475	2,810	416	3,701	360	300	286	2,503	252
Hertfordshire	780	5,332	539	6,688	564	418	456	4,878	372
Humberside	814	3,547	518	4,879	764	671	386	2,786	272
Isle of Wight	131	581	113	825	102	94	88	481	60
Kent	1,237	6,272	797	8,475	1,117	631	767	5,555	405
Lancashire	1,531	6,700	907	9,168	1,374	650	470	6,115	559
Leicestershire	700	3,703	445	4,918	648	439	326	3,232	273
Lincolnshire	502	2,899	412	3,813	321	293	306	2,668	225
Merseyside	1,596	7,171	884	9,651	1,493	588	316	6,582	672
Norfolk	559	2,740	498	3,906	381	302	343	2,645	235
Northamptonshire	420	2,386	249	3,055	357	192	186	2,184	136
Northumberland	267	1,200	204	1,671	185	94	56	1,156	180
North Yorkshire	560	3,622	523	4,723	412	357	463	3,219	272
Nottinghamshire	874	4,162	551	5,920	831	542	410	3,695	442
Oxfordshire	317	2,459	295	3,212	269	309	252	2,164	218
Shropshire	286	1,724	259	2,269	219	168	150	1,568	164
Somerset	284	1,730	335	2,370	225	194	167	1,707	77
South Yorkshire	1,092	4,601	653	6,429	1,095	370	306	4,085	573
Staffordshire	964	5,149	603	6,888	801	436	435	4,780	436
Suffolk	364	2,293	303	3,018	271	272	271	2,013	191
Surrey	660	5,826	711	7,623	595	535	729	5,465	299
Tyne & Wear	893	3,627	560	5,080	1,073	337	141	3,122	407
Warwickshire	431	2,610	294	3,493	298	218	271	2,432	274
West Midlands	2,276	8,914	1,175	12,366	2,588	880	612	7,547	739
West Sussex	523	3,032	517	4,072	366	459	312	2,691	244
West Yorkshire	2,104	9,564	1,193	12,861	2,184	689	529	8,513	946
Wiltshire	408	2,525	328	3,302	322	231	280	2,269	200
England	38,714	212,071	27,258	283,753	40,012	22,474	21,478	181,425	18,364
Wales	2,296	10,979	1,575	14,853	2,047	764	716	10,388	938
Scotland	3,825	15,325	2,542	21,696	4,322	1,296	850	13,464	1,764
Great Britain	44,835	238,375	31,375	320,302	46,381	24,534	23,044	205,277	21,066
Northern Ireland	1,869	9,659	1,047	12,575	1,256	359	239	9,422	1,299
United Kingdom	46,704	248,034	32,422	332,877	47,637	24,893	23,283	214,699	22,365

1 Includes age not reported.
2 Includes road user type not reported.

3 Number of casualties: by county and road user type: 1981-85 average[1]

Number of casualties

	Children (0-15)	Adults (16-59)	Older adults (60+)	All[2] casualties	Pedest-rians	Pedal cyclists	Motor cyclists	Car occupants	Other[3] road users
Avon	616	3,520	447	4,584	777	402	1,399	1,768	238
Bedfordshire	502	2,480	252	3,235	495	299	628	1,552	262
Berkshire	573	3,232	333	4,243	567	449	904	2,167	157
Buckinghamshire	464	2,713	283	3,504	409	287	700	1,940	168
Cambridgeshire	489	3,095	397	3,981	345	646	923	1,834	233
Cheshire	803	3,789	490	5,095	711	593	1,126	2,324	341
Cleveland	587	1,853	231	2,671	682	274	515	1,016	185
Cornwall	359	2,079	253	2,691	339	151	756	1,301	144
Cumbria	441	2,068	297	2,806	444	216	606	1,383	157
Derbyshire	715	3,505	439	4,933	808	405	1,207	2,098	415
Devon	769	4,333	624	5,726	845	400	1,654	2,526	302
Dorset	461	2,745	471	3,677	487	396	959	1,647	188
Durham	450	1,806	221	2,476	510	140	412	1,216	198
East Sussex	535	2,722	655	3,911	725	287	830	1,842	227
Essex	1,344	7,165	947	9,474	1,212	803	1,845	5,003	611
Gloucestershire	419	2,549	308	3,276	378	348	926	1,465	160
Greater London	7,106	37,831	5,855	54,156	13,081	4,739	9,957	21,778	4,601
Greater Manchester	2,946	9,320	1,431	13,699	3,931	1,376	2,284	5,186	922
Hampshire	1,276	7,151	881	9,308	1,159	1,182	2,530	3,981	456
Hereford & Worcester	491	2,895	384	3,770	461	370	847	1,909	183
Hertfordshire	784	4,401	485	5,729	738	511	1,173	3,003	304
Humberside	842	3,601	491	4,934	821	727	1,377	1,620	388
Isle of Wight	107	481	74	662	107	61	206	260	28
Kent	1,251	6,769	848	8,867	1,246	744	2,291	4,139	447
Lancashire	1,399	5,155	906	7,460	1,683	666	1,458	3,188	466
Leicestershire	752	3,657	415	4,825	827	507	1,117	2,124	249
Lincolnshire	501	2,866	382	3,749	365	381	852	1,929	221
Merseyside	1,632	4,718	875	7,225	2,066	583	1,009	2,926	642
Norfolk	551	3,195	495	4,241	483	456	1,063	1,999	240
Northamptonshire	499	2,818	334	3,652	449	240	779	1,913	271
Northumberland	215	1,142	159	1,516	192	95	270	828	131
North Yorkshire	568	3,349	496	4,413	531	420	1,030	2,150	283
Nottinghamshire	987	4,364	570	5,920	1,111	609	1,362	2,381	458
Oxfordshire	389	2,677	297	3,424	362	382	798	1,663	219
Shropshire	297	1,767	211	2,275	252	185	473	1,237	129
Somerset	299	1,875	276	2,450	267	222	640	1,204	117
South Yorkshire	1,108	4,121	685	5,914	1,475	354	1,069	2,308	708
Staffordshire	1,038	4,972	518	6,528	983	558	1,388	3,167	432
Suffolk	479	2,762	385	3,627	397	389	961	1,696	183
Surrey	921	5,844	779	7,640	808	838	1,764	3,918	312
Tyne & Wear	1,028	2,906	509	4,443	1,491	334	650	1,568	400
Warwickshire	400	2,179	261	2,839	339	295	606	1,446	154
West Midlands	2,714	8,345	1,227	12,286	3,596	1,064	1,993	4,812	820
West Sussex	498	2,919	527	3,943	440	464	907	1,953	180
West Yorkshire	2,039	7,531	1,084	10,654	2,728	722	2,048	4,386	770
Wiltshire	491	3,080	377	3,948	392	358	887	2,056	256
England	43,133	204,343	28,867	280,382	52,515	25,927	59,179	123,806	18,956
Wales	2,320	10,500	1,576	14,395	2,666	857	2,566	7,211	1,094
Scotland	4,881	19,157	3,097	27,134	6,560	1,607	3,446	12,924	2,598
Great Britain	50,334	234,000	33,540	321,912	61,741	28,391	65,191	143,941	22,647
Northern Ireland[4]	1,516	5,954	731	8,204	1,648	399	765	5,398	
United Kingdom[4]	51,850	239,954	34,271	330,115	63,389	28,791	65,956	171,986	

1 Figures have been rounded so there may be an apparent slight discrepancy between the sum of the constituent items and the total as shown.
2 Includes age not reported.
3 Includes road user type not reported.
4 It is not possible to give separate casualty figures for car occupants and other road users for Northern Ireland for these years.

4   Total casualty rates[1]: by county and road user type: 1996

	Children (0-15)	Adults (16-59)	Elderly (60+)	All[2] casualties	Pedest-rians	Pedal cyclists	Motor cyclists	Car occupants	Other[3] road users
Avon	266	534	203	413	64	36	43	244	27
Bedfordshire	314	658	233	509	62	34	36	345	31
Berkshire	300	604	233	501	52	52	41	336	20
Buckinghamshire	296	681	245	545	50	36	40	395	25
Cambridgeshire	369	788	289	620	48	92	52	392	35
Cheshire	402	901	308	678	63	48	41	476	51
Cleveland	365	542	203	436	87	39	11	277	22
Cornwall	325	707	231	512	63	32	44	346	27
Cumbria	418	700	277	548	66	43	40	360	40
Derbyshire	347	665	215	524	65	35	46	342	36
Devon	325	640	213	475	66	40	55	288	26
Dorset	342	706	272	522	48	45	45	350	34
Durham	391	590	229	474	73	24	19	316	41
East Sussex	392	694	298	534	88	44	45	322	36
Essex	348	722	254	575	67	43	45	387	33
Gloucestershire	304	617	251	475	49	43	48	308	27
Greater London	358	738	324	636	132	64	77	314	49
Greater Manchester	485	800	268	629	115	47	23	399	44
Hampshire	357	716	268	553	59	64	53	343	33
Hereford & Worcester	347	663	266	514	57	41	46	336	34
Hertfordshire	363	827	278	630	56	41	45	454	33
Humberside	444	668	267	536	86	82	53	278	36
Isle of Wight	387	663	313	512	76	58	61	277	40
Kent	337	646	226	501	65	37	53	322	25
Lancashire	492	790	310	626	97	47	37	401	43
Leicestershire	349	642	270	514	75	44	36	328	32
Lincolnshire	400	797	286	598	57	49	48	410	34
Merseyside	503	819	318	646	104	41	21	427	53
Norfolk	320	633	265	499	48	40	47	339	25
Northamptonshire	285	645	228	491	61	33	33	336	27
Northumberland	353	615	270	487	50	29	23	339	46
North Yorkshire	392	830	345	637	63	46	63	419	46
Nottinghamshire	436	666	244	570	85	45	45	347	48
Oxfordshire	275	637	259	511	44	58	49	325	34
Shropshire	315	696	280	531	51	35	35	370	41
Somerset	331	686	263	515	46	39	39	365	25
South Yorkshire	390	546	250	454	85	29	22	274	44
Staffordshire	401	765	295	626	71	44	43	422	47
Suffolk	275	529	221	409	46	43	41	257	23
Surrey	343	915	328	723	61	57	59	513	33
Tyne & Wear	378	503	218	417	94	30	9	249	35
Warwickshire	329	786	274	616	54	46	59	421	37
West Midlands	379	561	221	453	95	34	23	276	25
West Sussex	334	682	265	509	49	55	43	335	28
West Yorkshire	432	701	300	565	106	33	26	358	41
Wiltshire	320	710	279	545	55	44	47	361	39
England	374	698	270	557	82	47	44	347	37
Wales	375	659	264	512	70	26	28	355	33
Scotland	383	512	248	433	90	26	19	262	36
Great Britain	375	679	268	543	82	44	41	340	37
Northern Ireland	450	1,000	372	756	76	22	14	566	78
United Kingdom	377	688	270	549	82	43	40	346	38

1 Based on mid year 1996 population estimates.
2 Includes age not reported.
3 Includes road user type not reported.

5 Casualty indicators: by county and road user type: 1996

Percentage of all casualties

	Percentage of all casualties who are:							Other[2] road users
	Children[1] (0-15)	Adults[1] (16-59)	Elderly[1] (60+)	Pedest-rians	Pedal cyclists	Motor cyclists	Car occupants	
Avon	13.8	76.1	10.0	15.3	9.4	8.1	62.6	4.6
Bedfordshire	13.8	78.1	8.0	13.2	7.0	7.0	66.2	6.7
Berkshire	12.2	80.7	7.1	9.7	8.8	8.3	69.0	4.2
Buckinghamshire	12.3	79.6	8.1	7.7	5.9	6.3	74.9	5.2
Cambridgeshire	10.1	80.9	8.9	6.7	13.7	6.7	67.3	5.6
Cheshire	13.1	77.6	9.3	9.0	6.8	5.4	71.9	6.9
Cleveland	20.5	72.0	7.6	21.3	7.9	2.4	61.4	7.0
Cornwall	12.9	75.1	12.0	10.2	6.0	9.5	68.8	5.4
Cumbria	13.3	74.9	11.8	11.4	6.9	7.6	67.9	6.1
Derbyshire	13.5	76.8	9.7	11.3	7.4	7.6	66.8	6.9
Devon	13.5	74.7	11.8	13.2	7.0	9.2	64.8	5.7
Dorset	10.6	75.6	13.8	9.6	7.8	8.1	69.2	5.2
Durham	16.1	74.7	9.2	14.4	5.5	3.9	67.9	8.4
East Sussex	12.9	72.9	14.2	15.0	6.7	7.6	64.2	6.5
Essex	12.3	77.7	10.0	10.2	7.6	7.8	68.2	6.2
Gloucestershire	11.3	76.4	12.3	11.3	7.6	9.0	65.2	7.0
Greater London	11.7	79.3	8.9	20.2	9.5	12.9	49.8	7.6
Greater Manchester	16.7	75.3	8.0	17.7	7.5	3.1	64.9	6.8
Hampshire	12.6	76.7	10.7	10.5	10.8	8.9	64.0	5.7
Hereford & Worcester	12.8	75.9	11.2	9.7	8.1	7.7	67.6	6.8
Hertfordshire	11.7	80.2	8.1	8.4	6.3	6.8	72.9	5.6
Humberside	16.7	72.7	10.6	15.7	13.8	7.9	57.1	5.6
Isle of Wight	15.9	70.4	13.7	12.4	11.4	10.7	58.3	7.3
Kent	14.9	75.5	9.6	13.2	7.4	9.1	65.5	4.8
Lancashire	16.8	73.3	9.9	15.0	7.1	5.1	66.7	6.1
Leicestershire	14.4	76.4	9.2	13.2	8.9	6.6	65.7	5.6
Lincolnshire	13.2	76.0	10.8	8.4	7.7	8.0	70.0	5.9
Merseyside	16.5	74.3	9.2	15.5	6.1	3.3	68.2	7.0
Norfolk	14.7	72.2	13.1	9.8	7.7	8.8	67.7	6.0
Northamptonshire	13.7	78.1	8.2	11.7	6.3	6.1	71.5	4.5
Northumberland	16.0	71.8	12.2	11.1	5.6	3.4	69.2	10.8
North Yorkshire	11.9	77.0	11.1	8.7	7.6	9.8	68.2	5.8
Nottinghamshire	15.6	74.5	9.9	14.0	9.2	6.9	62.4	7.5
Oxfordshire	10.3	80.1	9.6	8.4	9.6	7.8	67.4	6.8
Shropshire	12.6	76.0	11.4	9.7	7.4	6.6	69.1	7.2
Somerset	12.1	73.6	14.3	9.5	8.2	7.0	72.0	3.2
South Yorkshire	17.2	72.5	10.3	17.0	5.8	4.8	63.5	8.9
Staffordshire	14.4	76.7	9.0	11.6	6.3	6.3	69.4	6.3
Suffolk	12.3	77.5	10.2	9.0	9.0	9.0	66.7	6.3
Surrey	9.2	81.0	9.9	7.8	7.0	9.6	71.7	3.9
Tyne & Wear	17.6	71.4	11.0	21.1	6.6	2.8	61.5	8.0
Warwickshire	12.9	78.3	8.8	8.5	6.2	7.8	69.6	7.8
West Midlands	18.4	72.1	9.5	20.9	7.1	4.9	61.0	6.0
West Sussex	12.8	74.5	12.7	9.0	11.3	7.7	66.1	6.0
West Yorkshire	16.4	74.4	9.3	17.0	5.4	4.1	66.2	7.4
Wiltshire	12.5	77.4	10.1	9.8	7.0	8.5	68.7	6.1
England	13.9	76.3	9.8	14.1	7.9	7.6	63.9	6.5
Wales	15.5	73.9	10.6	13.8	5.1	4.8	69.9	6.3
Scotland	17.6	70.6	11.7	19.9	6.0	3.9	62.1	8.1
Great Britain	14.0	74.4	9.8	14.5	7.7	7.2	64.1	6.6
Northern Ireland	14.9	76.8	8.3	10.0	2.9	1.9	74.9	10.3
United Kingdom	14.3	75.8	9.9	14.3	7.5	7.0	64.5	6.7

1 Percentage of casualties of known age.
2 Includes road user type not reported.

6 Casualty changes: by county and severity: 1981-85 average, 1996

Number of casualties

	Fatal and serious casualties			Total casualties		
	1981-85 average	1996	Percentage change	1981-85 average	1996	Percentage change
Avon	1,356	445	-67.2	4,584	3,669	-20.0
Bedfordshire	714	406	-43.2	3,235	3,069	-5.1
Berkshire	1,095	320	-70.8	4,243	4,124	-2.8
Buckinghamshire	1,031	440	-57.3	3,504	4,110	17.3
Cambridgeshire	1,087	782	-28.0	3,981	4,692	17.9
Cheshire	916	1,291	40.9	5,095	6,850	34.4
Cleveland	486	270	-44.5	2,671	2,536	-5.1
Cornwall	858	383	-55.3	2,691	2,809	4.4
Cumbria	829	518	-37.5	2,806	2,676	-4.6
Derbyshire	1,222	821	-32.8	4,933	5,139	4.2
Devon	1,897	729	-61.6	5,726	5,300	-7.4
Dorset	940	506	-46.2	3,677	3,904	6.2
Durham	703	377	-46.4	2,476	3,064	23.7
East Sussex	989	713	-27.9	3,911	4,453	13.8
Essex	2,398	1,409	-41.2	9,474	8,997	-5.0
Gloucestershire	1,166	375	-67.8	3,276	2,522	-23.0
Greater London[1]	8,230 (9,175)	6,826	-17.1	54,156	45,457	-16.1
Greater Manchester	2,362	1,310	-44.5	13,699	16,472	20.2
Hampshire	2,755	1,398	-49.3	9,308	9,534	2.4
Hereford & Worcester	1,071	840	-21.6	3,770	3,701	-1.8
Hertfordshire	1,388	1,135	-18.2	5,729	6,688	16.7
Humberside	1,129	802	-28.9	4,934	4,879	-1.1
Isle of Wight	184	160	-13.0	662	825	24.7
Kent	2,385	1,355	-43.2	8,867	8,475	-4.4
Lancashire	1,704	1,522	-10.7	7,460	9,168	22.9
Leicestershire	1,226	582	-52.5	4,825	4,918	1.9
Lincolnshire	1,074	785	-26.9	3,749	3,813	1.7
Merseyside	1,237	858	-30.6	7,225	9,651	33.6
Norfolk	1,524	840	-44.9	4,241	3,906	-7.9
Northamptonshire	1,328	785	-40.9	3,652	3,055	-16.3
Northumberland	400	282	-29.5	1,516	1,671	10.2
North Yorkshire	1,835	1,133	-38.3	4,413	4,723	7.0
Nottinghamshire	1,540	1,161	-24.6	5,920	5,920	0.0
Oxfordshire	1,067	359	-66.4	3,424	3,212	-6.2
Shropshire	833	543	-34.8	2,275	2,269	-0.3
Somerset	811	369	-54.5	2,450	2,370	-3.3
South Yorkshire	1,320	742	-43.8	5,914	6,429	8.7
Staffordshire	1,442	626	-56.6	6,528	6,888	5.5
Suffolk	1,170	513	-56.1	3,627	3,018	-16.8
Surrey	1,641	932	-43.2	7,640	7,623	-0.2
Tyne & Wear	1,048	644	-38.5	4,443	5,080	14.3
Warwickshire	1,059	717	-32.3	2,839	3,493	23.0
West Midlands	3,452	2,039	-40.9	12,286	12,366	0.7
West Sussex	922	606	-34.3	3,943	4,072	3.3
West Yorkshire	2,547	1,503	-41.0	10,654	12,861	20.7
Wiltshire	1,019	399	-60.8	3,948	3,302	-16.4
England	67,388	41,551	-38.3	280,382	283,753	1.2
Wales	3,855	2,130	-44.7	14,395	14,853	3.2
Scotland	8,887	4,390	-50.6	27,134	21,696	-20.0
Great Britain	80,130	48,071	-40.0	321,912	320,302	-0.5
Northern Ireland	2,362	1,676	-29.0	8,204	11,725	42.9
United Kingdom	82,492	49,747	-39.7	330,116	332,027	0.6

1 In September 1984 the Metropolitan Police implemented revised standards in the assessment of serious casualties.
Figures in brackets estimate casualty totals under standards prevailing since 1984. See preface.

7 Number of casualties: by road class, Government Office Region[1] and severity: 1996

Number of casualties

			Built-Up				Non Built-Up				All Roads[2]
		Motorways	Trunk	Principal	Other	Total	Trunk	Principal	Other	Total	
North East	Fatal	1	0	27	40	67	19	41	29	89	157
	KSI	22	9	311	659	979	132	225	215	572	1,573
	Total	164	125	2,679	5,762	8,566	989	1,464	1,168	3,621	12,351
North West	Fatal	34	5	88	74	167	34	56	32	122	323
	KSI	241	76	1,190	1,798	3,064	339	550	447	1,336	4,641
	Total	2,182	728	11,324	14,571	26,623	1,528	2,685	2,148	6,361	35,166
Merseyside	Fatal	1	1	27	30	58	1	1	5	7	66
	KSI	17	24	308	450	782	15	14	30	59	858
	Total	298	331	3,574	4,813	8,718	258	157	220	635	9,651
North West/Merseyside	Fatal	35	6	115	104	225	35	57	37	129	389
	KSI	258	100	1,498	2,248	3,846	354	564	477	1,395	5,499
	Total	2,480	1,059	14,898	19,384	35,341	1,786	2,842	2,368	6,996	44,817
Yorkshire/Humberside	Fatal	19	6	58	78	142	35	70	58	163	324
	KSI	120	80	826	1,643	2,549	354	642	515	1,511	4,180
	Total	1,092	618	7,383	12,798	20,799	1,539	2,850	2,612	7,001	28,892
East Midlands	Fatal	14	9	42	56	107	60	87	61	208	329
	KSI	102	117	655	1,205	1,977	475	880	700	2,055	4,134
	Total	738	768	4,487	7,952	13,207	2,119	3,721	3,060	8,900	22,845
West Midlands	Fatal	25	6	78	81	165	37	45	47	129	319
	KSI	218	77	1,094	1,786	2,957	372	593	625	1,590	4,765
	Total	1,513	688	7,839	11,588	20,115	1,853	2,482	2,754	7,089	28,717
Eastern	Fatal	17	4	28	77	109	82	78	84	244	370
	KSI	212	64	739	1,607	2,410	661	796	1,006	2,463	5,085
	Total	1,631	563	5,405	10,614	16,582	3,224	4,129	4,804	12,157	30,370
South East	Fatal	35	2	74	92	168	48	153	113	314	517
	KSI	269	51	1,263	1,956	3,270	374	1,239	1,131	2,744	6,283
	Total	2,834	603	10,213	15,927	26,743	2,357	7,432	7,062	16,851	46,428
London	Fatal	5	34	125	64	223	23	0	0	23	251
	KSI	77	646	3,363	2,524	6,533	182	12	22	216	6,826
	Total	647	4,489	22,439	16,761	43,689	854	127	140	1,121	45,457
South West	Fatal	9	8	51	55	114	53	119	73	245	368
	KSI	92	29	518	937	1,484	270	727	633	1,630	3,206
	Total	719	323	4,599	8,325	13,247	1,611	4,253	4,046	9,910	23,876
England	Fatal	160	76	598	647	1,321	392	650	502	1,544	3,024
	KSI	1,370	1,183	10,267	14,565	26,015	3,174	5,678	5,324	14,176	41,551
	Total	11,818	9,387	79,942	109,111	198,440	16,332	29,300	28,014	73,646	283,753
Wales	Fatal	2	5	22	67	94	60	38	22	120	216
	KSI	29	60	300	713	1,073	408	305	315	1,028	2,130
	Total	339	434	2,420	6,376	9,230	1,806	1,775	1,710	5,291	14,853
Scotland	Fatal	3	7	42	71	120	97	92	46	235	358
	KSI	64	97	674	1,429	2,200	706	783	637	2,126	4,390
	Total	447	564	4,121	8,432	13,117	2,636	2,950	2,568	8,154	21,696
Great Britain	Fatal	165	88	662	785	1,535	549	780	570	1,899	3,598
	KSI	1,463	1,340	11,241	16,707	29,288	4,288	6,766	6,276	17,330	48,071
	Total	12,604	10,385	86,483	123,919	220,787	20,774	34,025	32,292	87,091	320,302

1 Casualty data by road class are not available for Northern Ireland.

2 Includes speed limit not reported.

8 Casualty rates per 100 million vehicle kilometres: by road class, Government Office Region[1] and severity: 1994 - 1996 average

Rate per 100 million vehicle kilometres

| | | | A Roads | | | | | |
| | | | Built-Up | | Non Built-Up | | | All major roads[2] |
		Motorways	Trunk	Principal	Trunk	Principal	All A Roads	
North East	Fatal	0.4	0.4	1.0	0.5	1.2	0.9	0.8
	KSI	2.1	10.5	12.9	4.0	7.6	7.9	7.3
	Total	17.5	143.4	108.0	30.9	46.2	59.0	55.0
North West	Fatal	0.3	1.1	1.0	1.1	1.3	1.1	0.8
	KSI	2.2	15.8	14.5	9.5	12.5	13.0	8.8
	Total	19.6	127.8	133.8	44.1	58.1	95.1	65.9
Merseyside	Fatal	0.3	0.8	1.6	0.7	0.8	1.3	1.1
	KSI	2.1	10.1	18.0	5.4	8.0	14.3	11.3
	Total	31.0	164.1	203.0	61.2	68.4	163.8	131.0
North West/Merseyside	Fatal	0.3	1.0	1.1	1.0	1.3	1.1	0.8
	KSI	2.2	14.2	15.1	9.1	12.3	13.2	9.1
	Total	20.4	137.7	145.5	45.9	58.7	104.2	73.1
Yorkshire/Humberside	Fatal	0.3	1.0	1.0	0.8	1.6	1.1	0.9
	KSI	1.6	12.1	13.8	7.7	13.9	12.0	9.2
	Total	15.4	96.8	109.4	31.9	60.9	73.2	57.4
East Midlands	Fatal	0.2	1.0	1.2	1.0	1.6	1.2	1.0
	KSI	2.3	12.8	17.4	7.4	13.9	12.2	10.1
	Total	15.6	87.0	116.7	33.8	59.9	64.6	54.3
West Midlands	Fatal	0.2	1.1	1.1	1.1	1.4	1.2	0.8
	KSI	2.3	14.3	17.3	9.3	13.2	14.0	9.7
	Total	14.8	100.1	116.4	43.4	53.4	79.2	55.6
Eastern	Fatal	0.3	1.0	0.6	0.8	1.2	0.9	0.8
	KSI	2.6	15.8	14.4	6.0	11.3	9.7	8.1
	Total	21.7	116.0	105.3	29.8	55.2	55.9	48.1
South East	Fatal	0.2	1.1	0.7	0.7	1.1	0.9	0.6
	KSI	1.7	16.9	12.0	5.0	9.5	9.3	6.6
	Total	15.9	139.6	95.4	30.8	54.7	63.5	46.6
London	Fatal	0.3	1.0	1.1	0.4	0.5	1.0	0.9
	KSI	4.2	19.6	29.6	5.7	8.5	23.5	21.4
	Total	31.9	144.9	205.5	33.7	58.0	164.0	149.9
South West	Fatal	0.3	1.2	0.8	0.9	1.4	1.1	0.9
	KSI	2.1	10.5	9.1	5.0	9.7	8.2	6.9
	Total	13.9	111.2	78.7	28.6	53.0	54.2	45.5
England	Fatal	0.2	1.0	1.0	0.8	1.3	1.0	0.8
	KSI	2.1	16.2	16.7	6.5	11.1	12.0	9.3
	Total	17.5	124.8	127.9	33.2	55.4	78.5	61.7
Wales	Fatal	0.2	0.9	0.9	1.2	1.4	1.1	1.0
	KSI	1.5	9.1	10.3	9.0	10.0	9.6	8.3
	Total	13.7	64.0	83.8	41.4	54.6	57.9	50.8
Scotland	Fatal	0.3	0.7	0.8	1.3	1.5	1.2	1.1
	KSI	2.6	10.6	15.5	9.9	13.7	12.6	11.0
	Total	13.0	53.6	79.6	32.9	48.3	51.1	45.1
Great Britain	Fatal	0.2	1.0	1.0	0.9	1.3	1.1	0.8
	KSI	2.1	15.0	16.3	7.1	11.3	12.0	9.4
	Total	17.1	112.1	122.2	33.8	54.6	74.5	59.7

1 Casualty and traffic data by road class are not available for Northern Ireland.
2 Includes road class and type not reported.

9 Accident rates per 100 million vehicle kilometres: by road class, Government Office Region[1] and severity: 1994 - 1996 average

Rate per 100 million vehicle kilometres

| | | Motorways | A Roads | | | | All A Roads | All major roads[2] |
| | | | Built-Up | | Non Built-Up | | | |
			Trunk	Principal	Trunk	Principal		
North East	Fatal	0.4	0.5	1.0	0.4	1.1	0.9	0.8
	Fatal or serious	1.8	11.6	12.1	3.3	6.1	6.9	6.4
	All severities	11.2	123.7	80.5	18.3	28.9	40.5	37.8
North West	Fatal	0.2	1.0	0.9	0.9	1.3	1.0	0.7
	Fatal or serious	1.6	12.9	12.8	6.6	9.8	10.7	7.2
	All severities	11.7	84.2	94.7	25.6	37.6	65.2	44.6
Merseyside	Fatal	0.2	0.7	1.5	0.7	0.9	1.3	1.0
	Fatal or serious	1.9	8.3	15.9	4.1	6.1	12.5	10.0
	All severities	19.6	98.1	135.8	33.0	44.2	107.8	86.8
North West/Merseyside	Fatal	0.2	0.9	1.0	0.8	1.3	1.0	0.8
	Fatal or serious	1.6	11.6	13.3	6.3	9.6	11.0	7.5
	All severities	12.3	88.2	101.7	26.4	37.9	70.9	49.3
Yorkshire/Humberside	Fatal	0.3	0.9	1.0	0.7	1.4	1.0	0.8
	Fatal or serious	1.5	9.9	12.8	5.5	10.3	9.9	7.8
	All severities	11.4	67.9	84.2	20.0	38.2	52.7	42.7
East Midlands	Fatal	0.2	1.0	1.1	0.9	1.4	1.1	0.9
	Fatal or serious	1.7	11.2	15.6	5.5	10.7	9.9	8.2
	All severities	10.1	64.8	89.1	20.3	38.6	44.6	37.6
West Midlands	Fatal	0.2	1.0	1.1	1.0	1.3	1.1	0.8
	Fatal or serious	1.8	11.8	15.1	6.8	9.9	11.4	8.0
	All severities	9.3	68.7	86.4	27.6	35.3	56.3	39.6
Eastern	Fatal	0.3	0.8	0.6	0.7	1.0	0.8	0.7
	Fatal or serious	2.1	12.4	13.4	4.8	8.4	8.0	6.7
	All severities	14.1	75.3	83.9	19.5	35.2	39.8	34.1
South East	Fatal	0.2	1.0	0.7	0.6	1.0	0.8	0.6
	Fatal or serious	1.3	14.6	11.4	3.8	7.6	7.9	5.6
	All severities	10.3	104.2	77.7	19.3	36.4	46.4	33.7
London	Fatal	0.3	1.0	1.1	0.4	0.5	0.9	0.9
	Fatal or serious	3.4	17.3	27.1	4.7	7.7	21.4	19.5
	All severities	24.6	118.0	175.7	25.5	47.0	138.9	127.1
South West	Fatal	0.2	0.8	0.8	0.7	1.2	0.9	0.8
	Fatal or serious	1.3	8.4	8.2	3.6	7.4	6.6	5.4
	All severities	8.1	76.2	63.0	18.1	34.1	38.5	31.6
England	Fatal	0.2	0.9	0.9	0.7	1.2	0.9	0.8
	Fatal or serious	1.7	13.8	15.2	4.9	8.6	10.2	7.9
	All severities	11.3	93.5	100.8	21.0	35.9	57.9	45.4
Wales	Fatal	0.2	0.8	0.9	1.0	1.2	1.0	0.9
	Fatal or serious	1.3	7.6	9.1	6.2	7.6	7.5	6.5
	All severities	9.9	44.3	61.5	24.2	33.8	38.2	34.0
Scotland	Fatal	0.2	0.8	0.7	1.1	1.3	1.0	0.9
	Fatal or serious	2.1	11.0	13.9	6.8	10.0	9.9	8.7
	All severities	8.7	47.3	62.6	19.7	30.8	36.1	31.9
Great Britain	Fatal	0.2	0.9	0.9	0.8	1.2	1.0	0.8
	Fatal or serious	1.7	13.0	14.8	5.2	8.7	10.0	7.9
	All severities	11.1	85.2	96.0	21.0	35.3	54.6	43.6

1 Casualty and traffic data by road class are not available for Northern Ireland.

2 Includes road class and type not reported.

29

10 Accidents and accident indices[1]: by month, severity and Government Office Region: 1996

Index/number

	Jan	Feb	Mar	Apr	May	Jun	Jul	Aug	Sep	Oct	Nov	Dec	All Accidents
North East													
Fatal or Serious	95	110	92	80	92	94	91	105	110	105	135	91	1,382
All severities	91	101	87	91	97	98	94	97	101	109	129	106	8,690
North West													
Fatal or Serious	91	95	89	100	96	97	90	112	103	113	113	102	3,911
All severities	84	98	87	106	96	102	98	98	103	110	117	103	24,788
Merseyside													
Fatal or Serious	102	96	88	121	98	103	90	93	83	120	117	90	749
All severities	92	106	89	105	96	97	91	103	95	110	120	98	6,593
North West/Merseyside													
Fatal or Serious	93	95	89	103	96	98	90	109	99	114	113	100	4,660
All severities	85	100	87	106	96	101	97	99	101	110	118	102	31,381
Yorkshire/Humberside													
Fatal or Serious	81	92	74	96	98	97	112	107	108	111	113	112	3,512
All severities	87	105	88	89	93	99	100	99	96	111	122	111	20,843
East Midlands													
Fatal or Serious	89	93	81	101	91	89	91	109	108	118	117	113	3,377
All severities	92	100	87	95	92	97	92	99	99	118	118	112	16,123
West Midlands													
Fatal or Serious	96	93	85	96	94	109	100	102	98	118	106	103	3,941
All severities	88	101	89	94	95	102	101	96	99	114	114	108	20,796
Eastern													
Fatal or Serious	103	101	87	88	88	107	93	106	94	111	120	104	4,202
All severities	97	109	87	88	91	92	96	95	101	114	124	108	21,819
South East													
Fatal or Serious	97	84	81	89	90	106	100	102	105	118	120	106	5,341
All severities	88	95	84	89	93	101	102	96	106	116	124	105	34,090
London													
Fatal or Serious	96	93	86	89	93	88	103	106	110	118	122	95	6,098
All severities	90	104	97	95	102	98	104	95	103	111	114	89	38,356
South West													
Fatal or Serious	86	89	90	98	93	115	106	113	117	111	96	85	2,682
All severities	85	98	86	92	98	102	107	107	103	108	114	100	17,497
England													
Fatal or Serious	94	93	84	94	93	100	99	106	105	115	116	102	35,195
All severities	89	101	89	94	96	99	100	98	102	112	119	103	209,595
Wales													
Fatal or Serious	76	90	99	81	117	99	99	104	110	93	130	100	1,758
All severities	80	89	92	99	101	102	109	102	99	110	118	98	10,288
Scotland													
Fatal or Serious	81	94	91	91	96	98	100	110	119	106	109	107	3,623
All severities	80	95	86	93	97	95	95	111	108	113	123	105	16,056
Great Britain													
Fatal or Serious	92	93	86	93	94	100	99	107	106	113	116	102	40,576
All severities	88	100	89	94	96	99	100	99	102	112	119	103	235,939
Northern Ireland													
Fatal or Serious	98	102	77	108	96	89	94	97	121	117	102	100	1,285
All severities	91	108	78	99	103	92	84	95	118	109	127	97	7,093
United Kingdom													
Fatal or Serious	92	93	85	93	94	99	99	106	107	113	115	102	41,861
All severities	88	101	88	94	96	99	100	99	102	112	120	103	243,032

1 The base (= 100) is the average number of accidents per day for the region.

11 Accidents on motorways: by carriageway type, junction, number of lanes, Government Office Region[1] and severity: 1996

Number of accidents

		Junction			Non-junction		
		2 lanes	3+ lanes	Circular section of roundabouts	2 lanes	3+ lanes	Total[2]
North East	Fatal or serious	3	1	0	10	2	16
	All severities	9	2	2	49	6	76
North West	Fatal or serious	6	16	1	13	136	180
	All severities	86	98	39	115	865	1,306
Merseyside	Fatal or serious	0	1	0	3	12	16
	All severities	15	11	52	14	87	184
North West/Merseyside	Fatal or serious	6	17	1	16	148	196
	All severities	101	109	91	129	952	1,490
Yorkshire/Humberside	Fatal or serious	3	7	4	8	60	85
	All severities	35	33	56	63	406	638
East Midlands	Fatal or serious	0	8	3	1	53	66
	All severities	6	32	21	9	368	458
West Midlands	Fatal or serious	1	20	2	13	109	152
	All severities	10	73	19	55	658	879
Eastern	Fatal or serious	2	7	2	27	117	166
	All severities	32	73	7	123	682	1,014
South East	Fatal or serious	6	12	2	17	161	210
	All severities	55	127	58	169	1,289	1,781
London	Fatal or serious	6	8	3	11	31	63
	All severities	70	78	6	98	213	477
of which:							
Inner London	Fatal or serious	2	0	1	0	2	6
	All severities	16	11	1	11	20	63
Outer London	Fatal or serious	4	8	2	11	29	57
	All severities	54	67	5	87	193	414
South West	Fatal or serious	0	5	1	3	56	69
	All severities	11	27	19	27	358	463
England	Fatal or serious	27	85	18	106	737	1,023
	All severities	329	554	279	722	4,932	7,276
Wales	Fatal or serious	1	0	0	10	15	27
	All severities	13	4	24	64	108	219
Scotland	Fatal or serious	5	4	0	28	10	50
	All severities	29	28	8	109	76	292
Great Britain	Fatal or serious	33	89	18	144	762	1,100
	All severities	371	586	311	895	5,116	7,787

1 Accident data by road class are not available for Northern Ireland.
2 Includes slip roads and carriageway type not reported.

31

12 Accidents on trunk A roads: by carriageway type, junction, number of lanes, Government Office Region[1] and severity: 1996

Number of accidents

	Dual carriageway					Single carriageway							Circular Section of round-about	All Trunk A Roads[6]
	Junction[5]		Non-junction			Junction[5]			Non-junction					
	Number of lanes[2]		Number of lanes[2]			Number of lanes[3]			Number of lanes[3]					
	2	3+	2	3+	All	2[4]	3	4+	2[4]	3	4+	All		
North East														
Fatal or serious	18	4	33	4	59	15	3	0	30	1	1	50	5	114
All severities	140	21	191	39	391	74	6	3	84	3	2	172	91	659
North West														
Fatal or serious	25	8	28	6	67	95	8	19	96	4	3	225	13	307
All severities	169	64	115	20	368	443	34	65	341	10	15	908	114	1,405
Merseyside														
Fatal or serious	6	9	7	1	23	1	0	2	1	0	0	4	6	33
All severities	58	63	44	18	183	61	2	14	15	1	6	99	79	362
North West/Merseyside														
Fatal or serious	31	17	35	7	90	96	8	21	97	4	3	229	19	340
All severities	227	127	159	38	551	504	36	79	356	11	21	1,007	193	1,767
Yorkshire/Humberside														
Fatal or serious	33	3	67	6	109	68	6	5	99	6	1	185	16	312
All severities	152	17	276	25	470	340	28	25	317	22	6	738	171	1,385
East Midlands														
Fatal or serious	56	4	65	7	132	107	10	10	135	4	12	278	35	446
All severities	228	26	301	25	580	468	30	41	421	9	24	993	279	1,855
West Midlands														
Fatal or serious	40	5	57	1	103	97	6	0	103	4	0	210	33	346
All severities	259	24	238	10	531	485	29	2	338	10	2	866	262	1,665
Eastern														
Fatal or serious	72	8	163	7	250	111	9	2	127	0	1	250	41	545
All severities	315	47	674	63	1,099	453	44	6	450	11	2	966	314	2,389
South East														
Fatal or serious	30	17	65	18	130	62	5	2	96	6	0	171	28	331
All severities	215	81	396	130	822	367	22	12	384	19	8	812	348	2,001
London														
Fatal or serious	98	108	63	113	382	159	13	45	68	4	7	296	28	709
All severities	579	629	361	466	2,035	1,118	118	214	386	23	52	1,911	314	4,294
of which:														
Inner														
Fatal or serious	29	38	12	26	105	79	7	31	27	1	1	146	4	257
All severities	190	230	54	112	586	586	61	144	179	10	28	1,008	44	1,653
Outer														
Fatal or serious	69	70	51	87	277	80	6	14	41	3	6	150	24	452
All severities	389	399	307	354	1,449	532	57	70	207	13	24	903	270	2,641
South West														
Fatal or serious	20	3	34	4	61	54	4	1	73	13	0	145	12	219
All severities	107	19	202	16	344	343	17	7	317	26	1	711	179	1,238
England														
Fatal or serious	398	169	582	167	1,316	769	64	86	828	42	25	1,814	217	3,362
All severities	2,222	991	2,798	812	6,823	4,152	330	389	3,053	134	118	8,176	2,151	17,253
Wales														
Fatal or serious	19	0	49	1	69	83	10	0	159	13	0	265	9	345
All severities	93	5	196	5	299	354	30	0	528	36	0	948	85	1,339
Scotland														
Fatal or serious	54	10	100	15	179	91	5	2	264	3	7	372	13	568
All severities	206	26	359	51	642	397	14	13	735	9	19	1,187	77	1,918
Great Britain														
Fatal or serious	471	179	731	183	1,564	943	79	88	1,251	58	32	2,451	239	4,275
All severities	2,521	1,022	3,353	868	7,764	4,903	374	402	4,316	179	137	10,311	2,313	20,510

1 Accident data by road class are not available for Northern Ireland.
2 Number of lanes in each direction.
3 Number of lanes in both directions.
4 Includes one way streets.
5 Does not include accidents at roundabouts.
6 Includes unknown carriageway type and single track roads.

13 Accidents on principal A roads: by carriageway type, junction, number of lanes, Government Office Region[1] and severity: 1996

Number of accidents

	Dual carriageway					Single carriageway							Circular Section of round about	All Trunk A Roads[6]
	Junction[5]		Non-junction			Junction[5]			Non-junction					
	Number of lanes[2]		Number of lanes[2]			Number of lanes[3]			Number of lanes[3]					
	2	3+	2	3+	All	2[4]	3	4+	2[4]	3	4+	All		
North East														
Fatal or serious	48	7	43	6	104	164	10	11	157	6	9	357	16	480
All severities	324	57	204	34	619	1,069	49	60	648	27	22	1,875	328	2,848
North West														
Fatal or serious	86	49	54	22	211	644	55	58	423	10	20	1,210	31	1,468
All severities	898	423	334	110	1,765	4,496	306	536	1,814	53	119	7,324	384	9,704
Merseyside														
Fatal or serious	40	27	14	10	91	100	3	34	34	1	2	174	8	280
All severities	432	264	134	74	904	823	47	218	242	8	28	1,366	170	2,482
North West/Merseyside														
Fatal or serious	126	76	68	32	302	744	58	92	457	11	22	1,384	39	1,748
All severities	1,330	687	468	184	2,669	5,319	353	754	2,056	61	147	8,690	554	12,186
Yorkshire/Humberside														
Fatal or serious	112	28	59	18	217	451	27	20	409	16	4	927	52	1,201
All severities	698	203	375	74	1,350	2,910	215	153	1,746	56	38	5,118	594	7,118
East Midlands														
Fatal or serious	83	11	71	5	170	420	12	63	462	8	28	993	49	1,214
All severities	413	105	243	19	780	2,169	82	332	1,664	31	101	4,379	420	5,596
West Midlands														
Fatal or serious	152	37	110	8	307	501	24	24	456	6	11	1,022	47	1,378
All severities	916	205	451	57	1,629	3,130	115	130	1,678	36	32	5,121	609	7,383
Eastern														
Fatal or serious	78	9	105	7	199	456	34	5	454	16	2	967	90	1,265
All severities	437	51	465	47	1,000	2,659	160	35	1,827	71	25	4,777	1,011	6,856
South East														
Fatal or serious	131	13	158	21	323	835	33	31	721	8	6	1,634	124	2,112
All severities	943	162	784	113	2,002	4,936	258	185	3,335	95	52	8,861	1,583	12,720
London														
Fatal or serious	202	46	82	30	360	1,621	95	213	549	22	67	2,567	93	3,036
All severities	1,209	300	404	127	2,040	10,714	538	1,293	3,223	141	333	16,242	728	19,145
of which:														
Inner														
Fatal or serious	96	31	26	20	173	858	59	149	242	15	51	1,374	43	1,597
All severities	590	207	137	80	1,014	5,719	349	953	1,473	93	257	8,844	287	10,198
Outer														
Fatal or serious	106	15	56	10	187	763	36	64	307	7	16	1,193	50	1,439
All severities	619	93	267	47	1,026	4,995	189	340	1,750	48	76	7,398	441	8,947
South West														
Fatal or serious	58	8	61	8	135	355	15	4	412	7	4	797	52	989
All severities	393	64	325	38	820	2,595	104	46	2,092	55	18	4,910	530	6,309
England														
Fatal or serious	990	235	757	135	2,117	5,547	308	463	4,077	100	153	10,648	562	13,423
All severities	6,663	1,834	3,719	693	12,909	35,501	1,874	2,988	18,269	573	768	59,973	6,357	80,161
Wales														
Fatal or serious	30	3	16	2	51	182	14	6	220	8	7	437	15	506
All severities	174	19	101	7	301	1,028	65	36	1,092	23	21	2,265	218	2,798
Scotland														
Fatal or serious	48	16	58	14	136	340	10	33	579	8	36	1,006	16	1,178
All severities	308	89	295	68	760	1,682	44	260	1,974	27	141	4,128	228	5,173
Great Britain														
Fatal or serious	1,068	254	831	151	2,304	6,069	332	502	4,876	116	196	12,091	593	15,107
All severities	7,145	1,942	4,115	768	13,970	38,211	1,983	3,284	21,335	623	930	66,366	6,803	88,132

1 Accident data by road class are not available for Northern Ireland.
2 Number of lanes in each direction.
3 Number of lanes in both directions.
4 Includes one way streets.
5 Does not include accidents at roundabouts.
6 Includes unknown carriageway type and single track roads.

33

14 Accidents: by road class, severity, Government Office Region and county: 1981-85 average, 1995, 1996

Number

	Motorways			Trunk A roads			Principal A roads			All roads		
	Fatal	Fatal or serious	All severities	Fatal	Fatal or serious	All severities	Fatal	Fatal or serious	All severities	Fatal	Fatal or serious	All severities
North East Region												
1981-85	2	15	56	21	133	478	88	813	2,997	205	2,255	8,570
1995	6	16	105	9	89	617	60	463	2,787	135	1,309	8,309
1996	1	16	76	18	114	659	67	480	2,848	150	1,382	8,690
Cleveland[1]												
1981-85	0	0	0	4	19	97	18	174	770	42	423	2,137
1995	0	0	0	1	11	138	12	76	679	22	187	1,868
1996	0	0	0	7	19	110	19	86	611	37	230	1,919
Durham												
1981-85	2	10	35	7	40	110	24	195	585	55	577	1,801
1995	5	12	74	2	20	131	18	104	516	47	344	1,984
1996	0	12	50	4	24	129	21	100	568	45	329	2,020
Northumberland[1]												
1981-85	0	0	0	7	45	163	11	87	280	35	313	1,043
1995	0	0	0	3	35	141	9	68	326	16	206	997
1996	0	0	0	5	45	148	8	85	391	26	234	1,075
Tyne and Wear												
1981-85	0	5	21	2	29	107	36	357	1,361	73	942	3,588
1995	1	4	31	3	23	207	21	215	1,266	50	572	3,460
1996	1	4	26	2	26	272	19	209	1,278	42	589	3,676
North West/Merseyside Region												
1981-85	34	180	811	61	441	1,607	248	2,403	11,227	558	6,179	28,643
1995	24	181	1,386	44	328	1,720	173	1,895	12,212	387	4,879	31,020
1996	33	196	1,490	33	340	1,767	162	1,748	12,186	359	4,660	31,381
Cheshire												
1981-85	8	44	198	17	92	400	32	277	1,436	83	778	3,913
1995	3	48	387	13	111	420	36	388	1,763	74	1,027	4,602
1996	8	40	399	9	112	413	37	397	1,698	71	1,020	4,644
Cumbria												
1981-85	5	22	62	13	127	355	16	195	605	55	675	2,043
1995	3	20	85	14	80	343	17	150	573	50	442	1,899
1996	8	36	98	9	86	352	13	121	565	42	415	1,911
Greater Manchester												
1981-85	10	59	337	6	50	214	90	971	4,966	178	2,149	11,127
1995	10	50	546	4	17	219	54	538	5,315	110	1,226	11,917
1996	8	46	568	3	17	233	58	518	5,222	106	1,186	11,932
Lancashire												
1981-85	8	40	147	17	113	377	60	554	2,161	135	1,478	5,803
1995	5	48	220	7	86	391	42	522	2,178	94	1,451	6,155
1996	8	58	241	10	92	407	27	432	2,219	81	1,290	6,301
Merseyside												
1981-85	3	14	67	7	59	260	50	406	2,059	107	1,099	5,756
1995	3	15	148	6	34	347	24	297	2,383	59	733	6,447
1996	1	16	184	2	33	362	27	280	2,482	59	749	6,593
Yorkshire and Humberside Region												
1981-85	14	78	306	65	541	1,498	196	2,053	6,932	463	5,714	20,018
1995	14	90	560	41	303	1,344	119	1,318	6,943	313	3,709	19,954
1996	15	85	638	35	312	1,385	119	1,201	7,118	292	3,512	20,843
Humberside												
1981-85	2	10	33	8	72	243	28	308	1,201	73	996	3,894
1995	0	6	28	7	34	187	21	224	1,020	64	758	3,685
1996	1	7	42	5	45	206	23	213	968	63	700	3,742
North Yorkshire												
1981-85	0	3	8	24	239	467	29	474	1,048	82	1,423	3,128
1995	1	2	5	20	163	510	29	300	1,097	77	872	3,194
1996	0	1	6	15	149	465	25	288	1,132	71	861	3,274

1 This county contains no motorways.

14 Accidents: by road class, severity, Government Office Region and county: 1981-85 average, 1995, 1996

Number

	Motorways			Trunk A roads			Principal A roads			All roads		
	Fatal	Fatal or serious	All severities	Fatal	Fatal or serious	All severities	Fatal	Fatal or serious	All severities	Fatal	Fatal or serious	All severities
South Yorkshire												
1981-85	4	26	110	10	75	250	42	420	1,654	103	1,123	4,631
1995	5	39	184	2	25	137	21	234	1,595	53	644	4,374
1996	8	19	209	7	36	168	25	216	1,568	62	641	4,737
West Yorkshire												
1981-85	7	39	155	23	155	538	96	851	3,030	205	2,172	8,365
1995	8	43	343	12	81	510	48	560	3,231	119	1,435	8,701
1996	6	58	381	8	82	546	46	484	3,450	96	1,310	9,090
East Midlands Region												
1981-85	15	129	390	97	792	2,350	158	1,770	5,721	443	5,334	17,379
1995	9	80	393	69	486	1,967	123	1,188	5,397	340	3,466	15,902
1996	13	66	458	63	446	1,855	112	1,214	5,596	297	3,377	16,123
Derbyshire												
1981-85	2	18	69	20	159	545	34	339	1,130	97	1,057	3,743
1995	2	13	117	5	102	522	20	218	1,083	52	728	3,554
1996	7	18	154	14	80	452	20	227	1,121	59	689	3,569
Leicestershire												
1981-85	6	24	93	16	115	360	32	330	1,198	93	1,042	3,702
1995	4	30	149	16	53	286	14	154	1,157	69	511	3,515
1996	4	14	162	10	44	264	18	161	1,223	61	487	3,632
Lincolnshire[1]												
1981-85	0	0	0	20	160	454	29	294	932	76	852	2,683
1995	0	0	0	13	71	299	36	226	953	76	574	2,531
1996	0	0	0	12	76	280	29	256	1,001	69	605	2,548
Northamptonshire												
1981-85	6	75	190	18	182	434	22	381	1,011	69	1,025	2,673
1995	3	33	85	10	110	303	14	245	849	42	638	2,104
1996	2	24	88	9	90	260	15	241	840	35	588	2,086
Nottinghamshire												
1981-85	1	11	38	22	175	557	41	426	1,450	108	1,359	4,577
1995	0	4	42	25	150	557	39	345	1,355	101	1,015	4,198
1996	0	10	54	18	156	599	30	329	1,411	73	1,008	4,288
Eastern Region												
1981-85	15	116	440	101	840	2,481	172	2,170	7,213	480	6,885	22,569
1995	19	138	974	95	573	2,383	103	1,288	6,678	340	4,248	21,074
1996	16	166	1,014	72	545	2,389	98	1,265	6,856	334	4,202	21,819
Bedfordshire												
1981-85	4	29	109	10	94	345	17	160	622	50	600	2,444
1995	3	17	117	18	63	310	6	88	528	42	334	1,951
1996	1	10	112	11	60	327	12	94	552	36	344	2,225
Cambridgeshire												
1981-85	1	5	19	23	158	462	25	303	1,009	75	908	2,979
1995	0	1	12	28	135	557	21	186	1,015	72	615	3,197
1996	1	8	28	15	130	574	21	193	1,092	62	642	3,426
Essex												
1981-85	3	29	109	11	97	321	53	675	2,398	125	2,032	6,976
1995	9	45	291	10	89	450	27	382	2,187	85	1,285	6,769
1996	7	52	282	11	86	458	26	356	2,145	84	1,226	6,673
Hertfordshire												
1981-85	7	53	203	16	121	404	30	393	1,469	84	1,177	4,316
1995	7	75	554	5	88	390	19	251	1,395	42	870	4,493
1996	7	96	592	8	85	352	14	286	1,442	51	946	4,710
Norfolk[1]												
1981-85	0	0	0	21	190	461	27	360	910	82	1,207	3,110
1995	0	0	0	22	129	356	24	262	922	67	753	2,652
1996	0	0	0	13	102	317	12	216	931	48	644	2,644

1 This county contains no motorways.

14 Accidents: by road class, severity, Government Office Region and county: 1981-85 average, 1995, 1996

Number

	Motorways			Trunk A roads			Principal A roads			All roads		
	Fatal	Fatal or serious	All severities	Fatal	Fatal or serious	All severities	Fatal	Fatal or serious	All severities	Fatal	Fatal or serious	All severities
Suffolk[1]												
1981-85	0	0	0	20	179	488	19	280	805	64	960	2,744
1995	0	0	0	12	69	320	6	119	631	32	391	2,012
1996	0	0	0	14	82	361	13	120	694	53	400	2,141
South East Region												
1981-85	34	243	771	112	836	2,563	308	3,818	13,093	740	10,169	34,809
1995	26	249	1,740	56	396	2,115	189	2,041	11,948	431	5,295	32,037
1996	32	210	1,781	44	331	2,001	206	2,112	12,720	474	5,341	34,090
Berkshire												
1981-85	10	69	215	7	61	195	24	321	1,167	71	942	3,263
1995	3	31	292	2	7	122	10	104	1,074	32	293	3,007
1996	9	24	290	0	8	104	9	94	1,145	31	281	3,039
Buckinghamshire												
1981-85	5	38	120	3	36	110	27	318	1,001	63	843	2,617
1995	2	26	204	2	16	144	18	115	817	39	322	2,561
1996	4	25	218	4	13	149	18	128	955	50	360	2,891
East Sussex[1]												
1981-85	0	0	0	10	78	232	31	347	1,163	66	838	2,997
1995	0	0	0	2	62	248	19	203	1,122	37	510	2,916
1996	0	0	0	4	61	254	24	257	1,267	47	605	3,249
Hampshire												
1981-85	4	36	109	21	160	437	50	792	2,416	140	2,320	7,227
1995	7	61	358	10	82	329	26	416	2,233	68	1,160	6,834
1996	2	37	338	4	51	249	36	421	2,323	87	1,195	7,176
Isle of Wight[1]												
1981-85	0	0	0	0	0	0	4	70	214	8	155	495
1995	0	0	0	0	0	0	4	43	205	6	96	476
1996	0	0	0	0	0	0	6	58	233	9	129	576
Kent												
1981-85	7	49	162	21	175	539	63	779	2,543	142	2,053	6,819
1995	6	56	236	18	103	470	34	481	2,403	81	1,219	5,814
1996	7	38	261	14	92	481	38	490	2,530	82	1,157	6,263
Oxfordshire												
1981-85	1	6	12	24	164	521	26	279	801	71	871	2,531
1995	5	21	107	10	39	287	23	129	806	57	322	2,230
1996	6	19	125	12	46	291	18	109	791	55	294	2,304
Surrey												
1981-85	7	43	144	10	62	224	52	613	2,618	109	1,391	5,870
1995	2	50	516	6	39	256	40	329	2,232	72	843	5,444
1996	4	64	519	2	26	218	2b	346	2,268	63	808	5,557
West Sussex												
1981-85	0	2	9	16	102	306	31	299	1,170	70	757	2,990
1995	1	4	27	6	48	259	15	221	1,056	39	530	2,755
1996	0	3	30	4	34	255	31	209	1,208	50	512	3,035
London Region												
1981-85	6	35	266	56	413	2,489	301	4,269	25,584	521	7,588	45,274
1995	7	64	438	25	640	4,349	102	2,962	18,945	203	5,922	37,978
1996	5	63	477	53	709	4,294	122	3,036	19,145	242	6,098	38,356
Inner London												
1981-85[2]	..	..	..	..	..	..	..	..	..	212	3,383	20,946
1995	2	7	61	10	249	1,671	51	1,550	10,105	87	2,686	17,453
1996	1	6	63	12	257	1,653	67	1,597	10,198	104	2,707	17,531
Outer London												
1981-85[2]	..	..	..	..	..	..	..	..	..	309	4,204	24,327
1995	5	57	377	15	391	2,678	51	1,412	8,840	116	3,236	20,525
1996	4	57	414	41	452	2,641	55	1,439	8,947	138	3,391	20,825

1 This county contains no motorways.
2 Trunk road data not available for these years.

36

14 Accidents: by road class, severity, Government Office Region and county: 1981-85 average, 1995, 1996

Number

	Motorways			Trunk A roads			Principal A roads			All roads		
	Fatal	Fatal or serious	All severities	Fatal	Fatal or serious	All severities	Fatal	Fatal or serious	All severities	Fatal	Fatal or serious	All severities
South West Region												
1981-85	17	127	344	62	585	1,586	198	2,475	7,389	440	6,697	19,847
1995	19	78	478	31	212	1,232	147	1,059	6,196	319	2,843	17,272
1996	9	69	463	46	219	1,238	140	989	6,309	315	2,682	17,497
Avon												
1981-85	8	50	124	3	29	61	41	450	1,415	86	1,149	3,596
1995	8	32	210	3	7	56	30	168	1,091	61	459	3,144
1996	4	19	179	1	7	53	28	161	1,079	51	381	2,862
Cornwall[1]												
1981-85	0	0	0	10	92	249	14	236	667	39	696	1,984
1995	0	0	0	4	31	200	18	120	645	31	297	1,816
1996	0	0	0	8	40	217	15	106	695	33	302	2,021
Devon												
1981-85	2	10	27	13	131	345	35	570	1,563	82	1,568	4,354
1995	2	7	41	4	45	303	10	184	1,145	39	602	3,908
1996	0	9	48	8	56	317	22	187	1,238	50	622	4,010
Dorset[1]												
1981-85	0	0	0	4	45	148	23	311	1,112	48	803	2,779
1995	0	0	0	5	31	142	20	148	1,045	43	382	2,463
1996	0	0	0	6	27	151	16	161	1,109	43	411	2,710
Gloucestershire												
1981-85	1	21	54	13	145	369	24	282	705	59	967	2,479
1995	1	7	63	4	43	251	22	102	639	40	304	1,923
1996	2	15	70	10	43	217	19	109	634	46	307	1,876
Somerset												
1981-85	3	17	43	6	48	117	29	295	789	57	666	1,783
1995	4	7	52	3	10	58	24	164	748	51	339	1,737
1996	3	12	61	4	12	67	20	137	696	45	317	1,695
Wiltshire												
1981-85	4	28	96	12	94	297	32	331	1,138	68	847	2,871
1995	4	25	112	8	45	222	23	173	883	54	460	2,281
1996	0	14	105	9	34	216	20	128	858	47	342	2,323
West Midlands Region												
1981-85	19	137	476	80	639	1,827	191	2,263	7,415	484	6,527	21,030
1995	17	145	777	40	342	1,552	110	1,408	7,211	265	4,000	20,030
1996	24	152	879	41	346	1,665	115	1,378	7,383	299	3,941	20,796
Hereford and Worcester												
1981-85	4	29	104	10	83	245	31	329	1,060	71	859	2,762
1995	1	34	111	9	76	286	21	260	981	40	688	2,641
1996	7	20	103	13	99	308	20	237	959	61	661	2,630
Shropshire												
1981-85	0	2	4	14	147	363	17	170	473	51	653	1,611
1995	2	3	18	7	66	220	8	126	435	27	425	1,534
1996	1	4	21	10	79	248	12	139	466	35	435	1,627
Staffordshire												
1981-85	8	36	146	25	163	602	36	405	1,577	105	1,209	4,813
1995	6	14	203	9	73	554	28	197	1,713	69	536	4,708
1996	7	23	271	15	75	638	23	178	1,706	60	502	4,941
Warwickshire												
1981-85	4	29	68	19	148	336	23	220	553	77	850	2,078
1995	4	58	209	14	70	258	8	131	555	41	543	2,221
1996	5	49	218	2	51	279	10	164	638	41	583	2,395
West Midlands												
1981-85	4	41	154	12	98	280	84	1,140	3,752	180	2,956	9,767
1995	4	36	236	1	57	234	45	694	3,527	88	1,808	8,926
1996	4	56	266	1	42	192	50	660	3,614	102	1,760	9,203

1 This county contains no motorways.

14 Accidents: by road class, severity, Government Office Region and county: 1981-85 average, 1995, 1996

Number

	Motorways			Trunk A roads			Principal A roads			All roads		
	Fatal	Fatal or serious	All severities	Fatal	Fatal or serious	All severities	Fatal	Fatal or serious	All severities	Fatal	Fatal or serious	All severities
England												
1981-85	156	1,059	3,860	654	5,220	16,880	1,859	22,035	87,572	4,333	57,347	218,137
1995	141	1,041	6,851	410	3,369	17,279	1,126	13,622	78,317	2,733	35,671	203,576
1996	148	1,023	7,276	405	3,362	17,253	1,141	13,423	80,161	2,762	35,195	209,595
Wales												
1981-85	5	38	124	62	620	1,746	86	984	3,427	233	3,082	10,583
1995	4	28	209	49	323	1,382	75	502	2,956	193	1,677	10,275
1996	2	27	219	57	345	1,339	54	506	2,798	196	1,758	10,288
Scotland												
1981-85	16	110	265	138	1,010	2,433	228	2,751	7,438	581	7,412	20,471
1995	9	84	332	94	619	1,857	133	1,521	5,540	360	4,429	16,525
1996	3	50	292	85	568	1,918	118	1,178	5,173	316	3,623	16,056
Great Britain												
1981-85	177	1,207	4,249	854	6,850	21,058	2,173	25,769	98,436	5,147	67,842	249,192
1995	154	1,153	7,392	553	4,311	20,518	1,334	15,645	86,813	3,286	41,777	230,376
1996	153	1,100	7,787	547	4,275	20,510	1,313	15,107	88,132	3,274	40,576	235,939

15 Accidents and casualties by severity: vehicles involved by vehicle type: road length: all by selected individual motorways[1]: 1996

Number

	Accidents			Casualties			Vehicles involved				Kilo-metres open at December 1996[3]
	Fatal	Serious	All severities	Fatal	Serious	All severities	Two-wheel motor vehicles	Cars and LGV	HGV	All vehicles[2]	
England											
M1 / M10	21	136	1,088	24	194	1,825	52	2,236	316	2,635	310
M45	0	0	1	0	0	1	0	0	1	1	17
M2	3	6	66	3	10	105	3	101	28	134	43
M3	4	21	214	4	35	329	17	377	39	441	96
M4	9	52	567	9	68	861	39	1,093	129	1,282	186
M5	13	66	382	13	100	583	12	623	98	749	256
M6	36	140	1,050	38	210	1,854	32	1,928	425	2,409	386
M11	6	33	156	6	43	271	8	344	50	409	84
M18	3	1	49	5	5	76	1	89	26	119	46
M20	2	19	122	2	25	199	8	169	37	218	109
M23	0	10	91	0	10	155	10	187	8	205	27
M25	10	127	1,012	12	162	1,573	68	1,970	340	2,400	194
M26	0	0	11	0	0	16	3	10	5	19	16
M27 / M271 / M275	0	17	194	0	21	284	15	411	29	456	60
M40	9	39	288	10	64	470	2	454	80	538	147
M42	4	24	140	4	34	299	3	297	42	347	69
M50	0	0	12	0	0	20	0	16	2	18	35
M53	0	6	87	0	6	116	3	153	15	171	33
M54	1	3	30	1	7	42	1	46	7	54	37
M55	0	7	28	0	10	65	1	51	2	55	20
M56	2	9	124	2	13	223	6	234	23	263	60
M57	0	2	39	0	2	65	1	67	11	80	17
M58	0	5	18	0	5	23	1	28	0	29	19
M61	0	7	73	0	8	120	1	136	20	159	40
M62	9	63	597	11	77	993	10	1,144	217	1,381	175
M63	2	10	111	2	12	153	5	209	25	240	25
M65	0	5	50	0	8	73	0	91	4	95	22
M66	1	3	40	1	3	60	0	80	8	88	19
M69	0	1	34	0	1	55	2	56	3	61	28
M180 / M181	1	2	22	1	2	31	0	30	11	42	45
Other motorways	2	12	126	2	14	171	5	256	14	278	36
Motorways	138	826	6,822	150	1,149	11,111	309	12,886	2,015	15,376	2,657
A(M) roads	10	49	454	10	61	707	37	872	73	993	215
Total (inc A(M) roads)	148	875	7,276	160	1,210	11,818	346	13,758	2,088	16,369	2,872
Wales											
Motorways	2	25	216	2	27	336	12	449	57	521	..
A(M) roads	0	0	3	0	0	3	0	0	0	5	..
Total (inc A(M) roads)	2	25	219	2	27	339	12	454	57	526	117
Scotland											
Motorways	3	47	289	3	61	444	7	493	62	572	..
A(M) roads	0	0	3	0	0	3	0	2	3	5	..
Total (inc A(M) roads)	3	47	292	3	61	447	7	495	65	577	321
Great Britain											
Motorways	143	898	7,327	155	1,237	11,891	328	13,828	2,134	16,469	..
A(M) roads	10	49	460	10	61	713	37	874	76	1,003	..
Total (inc A(M) roads)	153	947	7,787	165	1,298	12,604	365	14,702	2,210	17,472	3,310

1 Casualty and accident data by road class are not available for Northern Ireland.
2 Includes pedal cycles, buses and coaches and other vehicles.
3 Excluding slip roads. Data for England from 1994 onwards supplied by DOT Statistics Directorate. Data for Wales from Welsh Office and Scotland from Scottish Office.

16 Distribution of accidents by road class and Government Office Region[1]: 1995, 1996

percentage (row sums = 100)

	Motorways		Trunk roads		Principal roads		Other roads	
	1995	1996	1995	1996	1995	1996	1995	1996
North East	1.3	0.9	7.4	7.6	33.5	32.8	57.8	58.8
North West	5.0	5.3	5.6	5.7	40.0	39.1	49.4	49.9
Merseyside	2.3	2.8	5.4	5.5	37.0	37.6	55.4	54.1
North West/Merseyside	4.5	4.7	5.5	5.6	39.4	38.8	50.6	50.8
Yorkshire/Humberside	2.8	3.1	6.7	6.6	34.8	34.2	55.7	56.1
East Midlands	2.5	2.8	12.4	11.5	33.9	34.7	51.2	50.9
West Midlands	3.9	4.2	7.7	8.0	36.0	35.5	52.4	52.3
Eastern	4.6	4.6	11.3	10.9	31.7	31.4	52.4	53.0
South East	5.4	5.2	6.6	5.9	37.3	37.3	50.7	51.6
London	1.2	1.2	11.5	11.2	49.9	49.9	37.5	37.6
South West	2.8	2.6	7.1	7.1	35.9	36.1	54.2	54.2
England	3.4	3.5	8.5	8.2	38.5	38.2	49.7	50.1
Wales	2.0	2.1	13.5	13.0	28.8	27.2	55.7	57.7
Scotland	2.0	1.8	11.2	11.9	33.5	32.2	53.2	54.0
Great Britain	3.2	3.3	8.9	8.7	37.7	37.4	50.2	50.7

1 Accident data by road class are not available for Northern Ireland.

17 Motor vehicles, population, area and road length (motorways and built-up and non built-up roads: by trunk and principal): by Government Office Region: 1996

Thousands/ number

	Motor vehicles currently licensed[1] (thousands)	Population[2] mid year (home) (thousands)	Area in hectares (thousands)	Road length (kilometres)				
				Motorways[3]	Built-up		Non built-up	
					Trunk	Principal	Trunk	Principal
North East	905	2,601	859	61	9	501	481	893
North West	2,453	5,471	1,351	521	114	1,431	664	1,523
Merseyside	484	1,420	66	62	24	311	44	60
North West/Merseyside	2,937	6,891	1,417	583	138	1,742	708	1,583
Yorkshire/Humberside	2,036	5,036	1,541	312	109	1,206	638	1,492
East Midlands	1,933	4,142	1,563	190	132	811	1,129	1,946
West Midlands	2,622	5,317	1,300	373	99	1,103	752	1,640
Eastern	2,744	5,293	1,912	251	71	1,007	1,258	1,867
South East	4,040	7,895	1,910	658	82	1,869	829	2,701
London	2,720	7,074	158	62	203	1,356	123	44
South West	2,540	4,842	2,383	299	44	1,154	982	2,893
England	22,477	49,091	13,042	2,788	886	10,749	6,900	15,059
Wales	1,264	2,921	2,078	126	194	880	1,388	1,812
Scotland	1,966	5,128	7,717	311	234	1,331	2,757	6,027
Great Britain	25,707	57,140	22,837	3,225	1,314	12,960	11,045	22,898
Northern Ireland	612	1,649	1,416	111	532[4]		1,718[4]	
United Kingdom	26,319	58,789	24,253	3,336	1,314	12,960	11,045	22,898

1 Includes all vehicles licensed to use public roads. From 1992, estimates of licensed stock are taken from the Department of Transport's Statistics Directorate Information Database.
2 Final 1996 population estimates.
3 Data for Wales from Welsh Office and Scotland from Scottish Office.
4 Trunk and Principal road length data are not available for Northern Ireland, data are for all A roads.

18 Motor traffic distribution between Government Office Regions[1]: by motorway and built-up and non built-up trunk and principal roads: 1994-1996 average

Percentage[2]

	Motorways	Built-up A		Non built-up A		All major roads
		Trunk	Principal	Trunk	Principal	
North East	1	1	3	5	5	3
North West	15	6	12	6	8	10
Merseyside	1	2	2	1	0	1
North West/Merseyside	17	8	15	6	8	12
Yorkshire/Humberside	9	7	9	8	7	8
East Midlands	6	11	5	10	9	8
West Midlands	13	8	9	7	7	9
Eastern	10	5	7	17	12	11
South East	25	5	15	13	21	18
London	3	33	15	4	1	7
South West	8	3	8	9	13	9
England	91	81	88	80	84	86
Wales	3	8	4	7	6	5
Scotland	5	11	8	13	10	9
Great Britain	100	100	100	100	100	100

1 Traffic data by road class are not available for Northern Ireland.
2 Figures have been rounded to the nearest whole number.

19 Motor traffic distribution between motorways, built-up and non built-up trunk and principal roads: by Government Office Region[1]: 1994-1996 average

Percentage[2]

	Motorways	Built-up A		Non built-up A		All major roads
		Trunk	Principal	Trunk	Principal	
North East	10	1	25	31	33	100
North West	39	2	30	12	17	100
Merseyside	25	6	50	12	8	100
North West/Merseyside	37	2	33	12	16	100
Yorkshire/Humberside	27	3	29	21	20	100
East Midlands	21	5	18	30	26	100
West Midlands	37	3	27	16	16	100
Eastern	23	2	17	34	25	100
South East	35	1	21	16	26	100
London	11	16	57	14	2	100
South West	22	1	23	23	32	100
England	27	3	26	21	22	100
Wales	16	5	22	32	24	100
Scotland	16	4	23	32	26	100
Great Britain	26	3	26	22	22	100

1 Traffic data by road class are not available for Northern Ireland.
2 Figures have been rounded to the nearest whole number.

HIGHWAYS AGENCY
TABLES

A1: Casualties: by Highways Agency Region and severity: 1981-85 average, 1989-1996; rate per 100,000 population, 1996

Number/rate

	1981-85 Average	1989	1990	1991	1992	1993	1994	1995	1996	Rate per 100,000 Population
Northern										
Fatal	1,429	1,378	1,331	1,241	1,158	1,072	942	977	931	6
KSI	17,736	15,231	15,218	13,393	13,068	12,058	12,408	12,481	12,073	78
Total	78,239	88,491	90,535	84,747	86,516	85,425	89,134	87,454	91,199	589
Midlands										
Fatal	1,356	1,371	1,363	1,136	1,089	970	1,008	953	924	7
KSI	19,751	16,343	15,956	13,293	12,666	11,634	12,321	11,375	11,353	92
Total	67,620	73,506	73,667	66,491	65,941	64,685	65,696	64,222	66,842	541
Southern										
Fatal	1,374	1,378	1,320	1,109	986	900	857	855	920	6
KSI	21,669	16,895	15,724	12,850	12,337	11,685	11,503	11,338	11,323	80
Total	80,363	83,176	81,282	73,081	72,958	73,355	76,984	76,876	80,443	567
London										
Fatal	539	460	409	368	316	286	270	210	249	4
KSI	8,229	9,344	8,923	7,868	7,226	6,413	6,171	6,482	6,802	96
Total	54,154	52,779	51,992	46,523	46,344	45,822	45,687	44,821	45,269	640

A2: Number of casualties: by Highways Agency Region and road user type: 1981-85 average, 1996

Number of casualties

	Children (0-15)	Adults (16-59)	Elderly (60+)	All[1] casualties	Pedest-rians	Pedal cyclists	Motor cyclists	Car occupants	Other[2] road users
Northern									
1981-85	14,773	54,863	8,315	78,239	18,074	6,905	15,060	32,194	6,006
1996	14,546	67,674	8,666	91,199	13,976	6,392	4,323	60,080	6,428
Midlands									
1981-85	10,507	50,615	6,436	67,620	10,843	6,728	14,715	31,120	4,213
1996	9,343	49,895	6,468	66,842	8,345	5,398	4,603	44,266	4,230
Southern									
1981-85	10,746	61,029	8,261	80,363	10,516	7,555	19,446	38,710	4,135
1996	9,827	60,776	8,325	80,443	8,523	6,375	6,673	54,585	4,287
London									
1981-85	7,106	37,830	5,854	54,154	13,081	4,739	9,957	21,776	4,601
1996	4,998	33,726	3,799	45,269	9,168	4,309	5,879	22,494	3,419

1   Includes age not reported.
2   Includes road user type not known.

A3: Total casualty rates: by Highways Agency Region and road user type: 1996

Rate per 100,000 population

	Children (0-15)	Adults (16-59)	Elderly (60+)	All[1] casualties	Pedest-rians	Pedal cyclists	Motor cyclists	Car occupants	Other[2] road users
Northern	93.9	436.9	55.9	588.8	90.2	41.3	27.9	387.9	41.5
Midlands	75.7	404.1	52.4	541.4	67.6	43.7	37.3	358.5	34.3
Southern	69.3	428.6	58.7	567.3	60.1	45.0	47.1	385.0	30.2
London	70.7	476.7	53.7	639.9	129.6	60.9	83.1	318.0	48.3

1   Includes age not reported.
2   Includes road user type not known.

A4: Casualty indicators: by Highways Agency Region and road user type: 1996

Percentage of all casualties

	Children[1] (0-15)	Adults[1] (16-59)	Elderly[1] (60+)	Pedest- rians	Pedal cyclists	Motor cyclists	Car occupants	Other[2] road users
Northern	16.0	74.5	9.5	15.3	7.0	4.7	65.9	7.0
Midlands	14.2	75.9	9.8	12.5	8.1	6.9	66.2	6.3
Southern	12.5	77.0	10.5	10.6	7.9	8.3	67.9	5.3
London	11.8	79.3	8.9	20.3	9.5	13.0	49.7	7.6

1 Percentage of casualties of known age.
2 Includes road user type not known.

A5: Casualty changes: by Highways Agency Region and severity: 1981-85 average, 1996

Number of casualties

	Fatal and serious casualties			Total casualties		
	1981-85 average	1996	Percentage change	1981-85 average	1996	Percentage change
Northern	17,736	12,073	-31.9	78,239	91,199	16.6
Midlands	19,751	11,353	-42.5	67,620	66,842	-1.1
Southern	21,669	11,323	-47.7	80,363	80,443	0.1
London	8,229	6,802	-17.3	54,154	45,269	-16.4

A6: Number of casualties: by road class, Highways Agency Region and severity: 1996

Number of casualties

	Motorways	Built-Up				Non Built-Up				All Roads[1]
		Trunk	Principal	Other	Total	Trunk	Principal	Other	Total	
Northern										
Fatal	62	16	210	230	456	99	179	135	413	931
KSI	424	231	2,777	4,852	7,860	902	1,567	1,320	3,789	12,073
Total	4,000	2,114	25,917	39,884	67,915	4,661	7,863	6,760	19,284	91,199
Midlands										
Fatal	42	16	138	184	338	169	204	171	544	924
KSI	362	200	2,003	3,526	5,729	1,364	1,982	1,916	5,262	11,353
Total	2,537	1,650	14,580	23,919	40,149	6,487	8,877	8,792	24,156	66,842
Southern										
Fatal	53	9	125	169	303	101	267	196	564	920
KSI	531	96	2,124	3,663	5,883	726	2,117	2,066	4,909	11,323
Total	4,822	983	17,006	28,547	46,536	4,330	12,433	12,322	29,085	80,443
London										
Fatal	3	34	125	64	223	23	0	0	23	249
KSI	53	646	3,363	2,524	6,533	182	12	22	216	6,802
Total	459	4,489	22,439	16,761	43,689	854	127	140	1,121	45,269

1 Includes speed limit not reported.

A7: Casualty rates per 100 million vehicle kilometres: by road class, Highways Agency Region and severity: 1994-1996 average

Rate per 100 million vehicle kilometres

	Motorways	Built-Up Trunk	Built-Up Principal	Non Built-Up Trunk	Non Built-Up Principal	All A Roads	All major roads[1]
Northern							
Fatal	0.3	1.1	1.1	0.8	1.4	1.1	0.9
KSI	2.0	14.0	14.4	7.2	11.8	11.8	8.9
Total	19.1	123.7	128.2	36.5	57.5	84.0	65.2
Midlands							
Fatal	0.2	1.0	1.1	1.0	1.5	1.2	0.9
KSI	2.0	12.6	15.9	7.2	12.9	11.5	9.0
Total	13.2	90.1	108.4	33.0	55.7	62.7	49.6
Southern							
Fatal	0.2	1.1	0.7	0.7	1.1	0.9	0.7
KSI	2.2	16.2	11.8	5.1	9.6	9.2	7.0
Total	18.8	133.3	94.4	30.6	53.8	61.7	48.3
London							
Fatal	0.2	1.0	1.1	0.4	0.5	1.0	0.9
KSI	2.9	19.6	29.6	5.7	8.5	23.5	21.3
Total	23.5	144.9	205.5	33.7	58.0	163.9	149.0

1 Includes road class and type not reported.

A8: Accident rates per 100 million vehicle kilometres: by road class, Highways Agency Region and severity: 1994-1996 average

Rate per 100 million vehicle kilometres

	Motorways	Built-Up Trunk	Built-Up Principal	Non Built-Up Trunk	Non Built-Up Principal	All A Roads	All Major Roads[1]
Northern							
Fatal	0.2	1.0	1.0	0.7	1.2	1.0	0.8
Fatal or Serious	1.5	12.2	12.9	5.1	8.7	9.6	7.3
All severities	11.5	87.8	92.2	21.5	35.2	57.4	44.1
Midlands							
Fatal	0.2	0.9	1.0	0.9	1.3	1.0	0.8
Fatal or Serious	1.4	10.9	14.0	5.2	9.5	9.1	7.1
All severities	8.0	65.5	81.9	20.1	35.1	43.2	33.9
Southern							
Fatal	0.2	1.0	0.7	0.6	1.0	0.8	0.6
Fatal or Serious	1.7	13.9	10.7	4.0	7.4	7.6	5.8
All severities	11.7	98.8	73.5	19.5	35.1	44.0	33.9
London							
Fatal	0.2	1.0	1.1	0.4	0.5	0.9	0.9
Fatal or Serious	2.3	17.2	27.0	4.6	7.2	21.2	19.2
All severities	17.7	117.8	175.0	24.9	44.1	137.8	125.1

1 Includes road class and type not reported.

A9: Accidents and accident indices[1]: by month, severity and Highways Agency Region: 1996

	Jan	Feb	Mar	Apr	May	Jun	Jul	Aug	Sep	Oct	Nov	Dec	All Accidents
Northern													
Fatal or Serious	90	99	83	99	97	95	96	107	105	111	116	102	10,243
All severities	87	105	87	98	95	99	97	99	99	110	120	106	64,483
Midlands													
Fatal or Serious	95	98	84	92	89	104	94	106	100	116	114	107	9,260
All severities	90	104	86	91	92	98	98	96	101	115	120	110	47,966
Southern													
Fatal or Serious	95	92	85	91	91	107	102	105	105	115	112	100	9,612
All severities	89	103	86	90	94	100	101	99	104	113	120	103	58,916
London													
Fatal or Serious	96	96	85	89	93	88	102	106	110	118	122	95	6,080
All severities	89	109	99	95	103	99	104	92	101	109	112	87	38,230

1 The base (= 100) is the average number of accidents per day for the region.

A10: Accidents on motorways: by carriageway type, junction, number of lanes, Highways Agency Region and severity: 1996

Number of accidents

	Junction			Non-junction		
	Number of lanes		Circular section of roundabouts	Number of lanes		Total[1]
	2	3+		2	3+	
Northern						
Fatal or Serious	12	25	5	34	227	315
All severities	150	152	151	242	1,498	2,358
Midlands						
Fatal or Serious	1	32	7	21	183	252
All severities	19	112	51	90	1,153	1,518
Southern						
Fatal or Serious	9	22	3	41	310	411
All severities	107	227	73	302	2,150	3,049
London						
Fatal or Serious	5	6	3	10	17	45
All severities	53	63	4	88	131	351

1 Includes unknown carriageway type and slip roads.

A11: Accidents on trunk A roads: by carriageway type, junction, number of lanes, Highways Agency Region and severity: 1996

Number of accidents

	Dual carriageway					Single carriageway							Circular Section of round-about	All Trunk A Roads[5]
	Junction[4]		Non-junction			Junction[4]			Non-junction					
	Number of lanes[1]		Number of lanes[1]			Number of lanes[2]			Number of lanes[2]					
	2	3+	2	3+	All	2[3]	3	4+	2[3]	3	4+	All		
Northern														
Fatal or Serious	87	24	149	20	280	191	18	26	264	11	5	515	47	846
All Severities	575	175	693	108	1,551	1,041	73	111	865	37	30	2,157	526	4,263
Midlands														
Fatal or Serious	141	14	224	6	385	298	24	12	338	10	13	695	90	1,175
All Severities	663	51	984	48	1,746	1,278	102	47	1,148	30	28	2,633	763	5,155
Southern														
Fatal or Serious	72	23	146	28	269	121	9	3	158	17	0	308	52	632
All Severities	405	136	760	190	1,491	715	37	17	654	44	8	1,475	548	3,541
London														
Fatal or Serious	98	108	63	113	382	159	13	45	68	4	7	296	28	709
All Severities	579	629	361	466	2,035	1,118	118	214	386	23	52	1,911	314	4,294

1 Number of lanes in each direction.
2 Number of lanes in both directions.
3 Includes one way streets.
4 Does not include accidents at roundabouts.
5 Includes unknown carriageway type and single track roads.

A12: Accidents on principal A roads: by carriageway type, junction, number of lanes, Highways Agency Region and severity: 1996

Number of accidents

	Dual carriageway					Single carriageway							Circular Section of round-about	All Trunk A Roads[5]
	Junction[4]		Non-junction			Junction[4]			Non-junction					
	Number of lanes[1]		Number of lanes[1]			Number of lanes[2]			Number of lanes[2]					
	2	3+	2	3+	All	2[3]	3	4+	2[3]	3	4+	All		
Northern														
Fatal or Serious	294	113	179	56	642	1,454	96	124	1,122	35	35	2,866	116	3,656
All Severities	2,402	952	1,092	295	4,741	9,773	626	969	4,876	154	208	16,606	1,562	23,273
Midlands														
Fatal or Serious	267	49	216	16	548	1,147	65	90	1,154	21	41	2,518	132	3,206
All Severities	1,513	327	856	85	2,781	6,730	340	491	4,431	108	149	12,249	1,454	16,552
Southern														
Fatal or Serious	227	27	280	33	567	1,325	52	36	1,252	22	10	2,697	221	3,525
All Severities	1,539	255	1,367	186	3,347	8,284	370	235	5,739	170	78	14,876	2,613	21,191
London														
Fatal or Serious	202	46	82	30	360	1,621	95	213	549	22	67	2,567	93	3,036
All Severities	1,209	300	404	127	2,040	10,714	538	1,293	3,223	141	333	16,242	728	19,145

1 Number of lanes in each direction.
2 Number of lanes in both directions.
3 Includes one way streets.
4 Does not include accidents at roundabouts.
5 Includes unknown carriageway type and single track roads.

A13: Accidents: by road class, severity, Highways Agency Region: 1981-85 average, 1995, 1996

Number of accidents

	Motorways			Trunk A roads			Principal A roads			All roads		
	Fatal	Fatal or serious	All severities	Fatal	Fatal or serious	All severities	Fatal	Fatal or serious	All severities	Fatal	Fatal or serious	All severities
Northern												
1981-85	53	291	1,241	167	1,274	4,129	566	5,608	22,286	1,323	15,206	60,973
1995	46	300	2,168	99	822	4,203	372	3,894	23,025	887	10,625	62,837
1996	56	315	2,358	100	846	4,263	368	3,656	23,273	860	10,243	64,483
Midlands												
1981-85	38	309	991	268	2,203	6,278	453	5,357	16,858	1,230	16,317	50,953
1995	33	258	1,352	198	1,204	5,078	315	3,264	16,066	863	9,457	46,343
1996	40	252	1,518	165	1,175	5,155	302	3,206	16,552	837	9,260	47,966
Southern												
1981-85	60	423	1,362	164	1,331	3,984	540	6,801	22,844	1,259	18,237	60,938
1995	58	442	3,014	88	703	3,649	337	3,502	20,281	783	9,690	56,539
1996	49	411	3,049	87	632	3,541	349	3,525	21,191	825	9,612	58,916
London												
1981-85	6	35	266	56	413	2,489	301	4,269	25,584	521	7,588	45,274
1995	4	41	317	25	640	4,349	102	2,962	18,945	200	5,899	37,857
1996	3	45	351	53	709	4,294	122	3,036	19,145	240	6,080	38,230

A14: Distribution of accidents by road class and Highways Agency Region: 1995, 1996

percentage (row sums = 100)

	Motorways		Trunk roads		Principal roads		Other Roads	
	1995	1996	1995	1996	1995	1996	1995	1996
Northern	3.5	3.7	6.7	6.6	36.6	36.1	53.2	53.6
Midlands	2.9	3.2	11.0	10.7	34.7	34.5	51.5	51.6
Southern	5.3	5.2	6.5	6.0	35.9	36.0	52.3	52.8
London	0.8	0.9	11.5	11.2	50.0	50.1	37.6	37.8

A15: Motor vehicles, population, area and road length (motorways and built-up and non built-up roads: by trunk and principal): by Highways Agency Region: 1996

Thousands/ number

	Motor vehicles currently licensed (thousands)	Population mid year (home) (thousands)	Area in hectares (thousands)	Road length (kilometres)				
				Motorways[1]	Built-up		Non built-up	
					Trunk	Principal	Trunk	Principal
Northern	6,338	15,489	4,080	995	308	3,643	2,025	4,303
Midlands	6,635	12,346	4,507	706	259	2,565	2,891	5,224
Southern	6,783	14,179	4,348	1,026	116	3,186	1,860	5,486
London	2,720	7,074	158	62	203	1,356	123	44

1 Excluding slip roads.

A16: Motor traffic distribution between Highways Agency Region: by motorway and built-up and non built-up trunk and principal roads: 1994-1996 average

Percentage[1]

	Motorways	Built-up A		Non built-up A		All major roads
		Trunk	Principal	Trunk	Principal	
Northern	30	23	33	26	26	29
Midlands	28	26	22	39	30	29
Southern	39	11	28	30	43	34
London	3	41	18	6	1	8

1 Figures have been rounded to the nearest whole number.

A17: Motor traffic distribution between motorways, built-up and non built-up trunk and principal roads: by Highways Agency Region[1]: 1994-1996 average

Percentage[1]

	Motorways	Built-up A		Non built-up A		All major roads
		Trunk	Principal	Trunk	Principal	
Northern	29	3	30	19	20	100
Midlands	26	3	20	28	23	100
Southern	31	1	22	18	28	100
London	11	16	57	14	2	100

1 Figures have been rounded to the nearest whole number.

ANNEX B

LOCAL HIGHWAY AUTHORITIES WITHIN EACH GOVERNMENT OFFICE REGION.

North East

Cleveland
Durham
Northumberland
Tyne and Wear

North West

Cheshire
Cumbria
Greater Manchester
Lancashire

Merseyside

Knowsley
Liverpool
St. Helens
Sefton
Wirral

Yorkshire and Humberside

Humberside
North Yorkshire
South Yorkshire
West Yorkshire

East Midlands

Derbyshire
Leicestershire
Lincolnshire
Northamptonshire
Nottinghamshire

West Midlands

Hereford and Worcester
Shropshire
Staffordshire
Warwickshire
West Midlands

South West

Avon
Cornwall
Devon
Dorset
Gloucestershire
Somerset
Wiltshire

Eastern

Bedfordshire
Cambridgeshire
Essex
Hertfordshire
Norfolk
Suffolk

London

City of London
Barking
Barnet

Brent
Bromley
Camden
Croydon
Ealing

Enfield
Greenwich
Hackney
Hammersmith
Harringey

Harrow
Havering
Hillingdon
Hounslow
Islington

Kensington and Chelsea
Kingston upon Thames
Lambeth
Lewisham
Merton

Newham
Redbridge
Richmond upon Thames
Southwark
Sutton

Tower Hamlets
Waltham Forest
Wandsworth
Westminster

South East

Berkshire
Buckinghamshire
East Sussex
Hampshire
Isle of Wight
Kent
Oxfordshire
Surrey
West Sussex

Government Office Regions

ANNEX C

LOCAL HIGHWAY AUTHORITIES WITHIN THE HIGHWAYS AGENCY NETWORK MANAGEMENT DIVISIONS

Northern

Cheshire
Cleveland
Cumbria
Derbyshire
Durham
Greater Manchester

Humberside
Lancashire
Merseyside
North Yorkshire
Northumberland

South Yorkshire
Tyne and Wear
West Yorkshire

Midland

Bedfordshire
Cambridgeshire
Gloucestershire
Hereford and Worcester

Leicestershire
Lincolnshire
Norfolk
Northamptonshire
Nottinghamshire

Oxfordshire
Shropshire
Staffordshire
Suffolk

Warwickshire
West Midlands

Southern

Avon
Berkshire
Buckinghamshire
Cornwall
Devon

Dorset
East Sussex
Essex
Hampshire
Hertfordshire

Isle of Wight
Kent
Somerset
Surrey
West Sussex

Wiltshire
London M25

London

City of London
Barking
Barnet

Brent
Bromley
Camden
Croydon
Ealing

Enfield
Greenwich
Hackney
Hammersmith
Harringey

Harrow
Havering
Hillingdon
Hounslow
Islington

Kensington and Chelsea
Kingston upon Thames
Lambeth
Lewisham
Merton

Newham
Redbridge
Richmond upon Thames
Southwark
Sutton

Tower Hamlets
Waltham Forest
Wandsworth
Westminster

HIGHWAYS AGENCY REGIONS

Definitions

Accident: Involves personal injury occurring on the public highway (including footways) in which a road *vehicle or pedestrian* is involved and which becomes known to the police within 30 days of its occurrence. The *vehicle* need not be moving and accidents involving stationery vehicles and pedestrians or users are included. One accident may give rise to several *casualties.* Damage-only accidents are not included in this publication.

"A" Roads: All purpose *trunk* roads and *principal* local authority roads.

Adults: Persons aged 16 years and over.

Built-up Roads: Roads with speed limits (ignoring temporary limits) of 40 mph or less. "Non built-up roads" refer to those with speed limits of over 40 mph. *Motorways* are included with non built-up roads unless otherwise stated. In tables where data for *motorways* are shown separately, the totals for built-up and non built-up roads exclude *motorway accidents*. In comparing such tables with those involving a built-up/non built-up split only, negligible error will be made by assuming that *motorway accidents* were all on non built-up roads.

Cars: Includes taxis, estate cars, invalid tricycles, three and four-wheeled cars, minibuses and motor caravans.

Casualty: A person *killed* or injured in an *accident*. Casualties are classified as either *killed, seriously injured* or *slightly injured.*

Children: Persons under 16 years of age.

Fatal accident: One in which at least one person is *killed* (but excluding confirmed suicides) and dies within 30 days of the accident.

Heavy goods vehicles (HGV): Prior to 1994 these were defined as those vehicles over 1.524 tonnes unladen weight and included vehicles with six or more tyres, some four-wheel vehicles with extra large bodies and larger rear tyres and tractor units travelling without their usual trailer. From 1 January 1994 the weight definition changed to those vehicles over 3.5 tonnes maximum permissible gross vehicle weight (gvw).

Light goods vehicles (LGV): Prior to 1994 these were defined as those vehicles not over 1.524 tonnes unladen weight. From 1 January 1994 the weight definition changed to those vehicles not over 3.5 tonnes maximum permissible gross vehicle weight. Light vans mainly include vehicles of the van type constructed on a car chassis.

Killed: Human *casualties* who sustained injuries resulting in death within 30 days of the *accident*.

KSI: Killed or *seriously injured.*

Licensed Vehicles: The stock of vehicles currently licensed on 31 December, when the annual census is taken at the Driver and Vehicle Licensing Agency (DVLA).

London: Where possible, data for London have been split into Inner and Outer London. Inner London comprises the City of London and the boroughs of Westminster, Camden, Islington, Hackney, Tower Hamlets, Lewisham, Southwark, Lambeth, Wandsworth, Hammersmith, Kensington and Chelsea, Newham and Haringey. Outer London is all other London boroughs, and includes Heathrow Airport. This definition conforms to that used by the Office for National Statistics (ONS).

Major Roads: These are *motorways*, A(M) and *A class roads* (both *trunk* and *principal*).

Motorcyclist: Riders and passengers of two-wheeled motor vehicles.

Motorways: Motorways and A(M) roads except where otherwise noted. The motorway lengths given in Tables 15 and 17 are main line lengths and exclude associated slip roads.

Motorway Accident: Accidents on *motorways* include those on associated slip roads and those at junctions between *motorways* and other roads where the *accident* cannot be clearly allocated to the other road.

Other Roads: These are "B" and "C" class roads and unclassified roads, including "road class not reported".

Pedal cycle: Includes tandems, tricycles and toy cycles ridden on the carriageway. Also includes battery-assisted cycles and tricycles with a maximum speed of 15 mph.

Pedal cyclist: Riders of *pedal cycles* including any passengers.

Pedestrians: Also includes persons riding toy cycles on the footway, persons pushing bicycles or pushing or pulling other vehicles or operating pedestrian-controlled vehicles, those leading or herding animals, occupants of prams or wheelchairs, and persons who alight safely from vehicles and are subsequently injured.

Population: The population data used in calculating rates are the final mid-1995 estimates. Mid-year estimates for 1996 were not available at the time of going to publication. The estimates include residents who are temporarily outside the country, and exclude both foreign visitors and members of HM armed forces who are stationed abroad.

Principal Roads: Roads for which County Councils (Regional and Island Authorities in Scotland) are the Highway Authority. The classified *principal roads* (which include local authority *motorways*) are those of regional and urban strategic importance.

Serious Accident: One in which at least one person is *seriously injured* but no person (other than a confirmed suicide) is killed.

Serious Injury: An injury for which a person is detained in hospital as an "in-patient", or any of the following injuries whether or not the *casualty* was detained in hospital: fractures, concussion, internal injuries, crushings, severe cuts and lacerations, severe general shock requiring medical treatment, injuries causing death 30 or more days after the *accident*. An injured *casualty* is coded as seriously or *slightly injured* by the police on the basis of information available within a short time of the *accident*. This generally will not include the result of a medical examination, but may include the fact of being detained in hospital, the reasons for which may vary from area to area.

Severity: Of an *accident,* the severity of the most severely injured *casualty* (either fatal, serious or slight); of a casualty, killed, seriously injured or slightly injured.

Slight Accident: One in which at least one person is *slightly injured*, but no person is *killed* or *seriously injured.*
Slight Injury: An injury of a minor character such as a sprain, bruise or cut which are not judged to be severe, or slight shock requiring roadside attention only.

Two-wheel motor vehicles: Mopeds, motor scooters and motor cycles (including motor cycle combinations).

Trunk Roads: Roads comprising the national network of through routes for which the Secretary of State for the Environment, Transport and the Regions in England and the Secretaries of State for Scotland and Wales are the highway authorities. The network contains both *motorways*, which legally are special roads reserved for certain classes of traffic, and all-purpose roads which are open to all classes of traffic.

Department of Transport

Accident Record Attendant Circumstances

1.1 Record Type

11 New accident record
15 Amended accident record

1.2 Police Force

1.3 Accident Ref No

1.5 Number of Vehicle Records

1.6 Number of Casualty Records

1.7 Date

Day Month Year

1.9 Time of Day

Hours Mins

24 hour

1.10 Local Authority

1.11 Location

10 digit OS Grid Reference number

Easting

Northing

1.12 1st Road Class

1 Motorway
2 A (M)
3 A
4 B
5 C
6 Unclassified

1.13 1st Road Number

1.14 Carriageway Type or Markings

1 Roundabout - on circular highway
2 One way street
3 Dual carriageway - 2 lanes
4 Dual carriageway - 3 or more lanes
5 Single carriageway - single track road
6 Single carriageway - 2 lanes (one in each direction)
7 Single carriageway - 3 lanes (two way capacity)
8 Single carriageway - 4 or more lanes (two way capacity)
9 Unknown

1.15 Speed Limit

mph

1.16 Junction Detail

00 Not at or within 20 metres of junction
01 Roundabout
02 Mini roundabout
03 T or staggered junction
04 Y junction
05 Slip road
06 Crossroads
07 Multiple junction
08 Using private drive or entrance
09 Other junction

Junction Accidents Only

1.17 Junction Control

1 Authorised person
2 Automatic traffic signal
3 Stop sign
4 Give way sign or markings
5 Uncontrolled

1.18 2nd Road Class

1 Motorway
2 A (M)
3 A
4 B
5 C
6 Unclassified

1.19 2nd Road Number

1.20 Pedestrian Crossing Facilities

00 No crossing facility within 50 metres
01 Zebra crossing
02 Zebra crossing controlled by school crossing patrol
03 Zebra crossing controlled by other authorised person
04 Pelican or puffin crossing
05 Other light controlled crossing
06 Other site controlled by school crossing patrol
07 Other site controlled by other authorised person
08 Central refuge - no other controls
09 Footbridge or subway

1.21 Light Conditions

1 Daylight: street lights present
2 Daylight: no street lighting
3 Daylight: street lighting unknown
4 Darkness: street lights present and lit
5 Darkness: street lights present but unlit
6 Darkness: no street lighting
7 Darkness: street lighting unknown

1.22 Weather

1 Fine without high winds
2 Raining without high winds
3 Snowing without high winds
4 Fine with high winds
5 Raining with high winds
6 Snowing with high winds
7 Fog or mist - if hazard
8 Other
9 Unknown

1.23 Road Surface Condition

1 Dry
2 Wet / Damp
3 Snow
4 Frost / Ice
5 Flood (surface water over 3cm deep)

1.24 Special Conditions at Site

0 None
1 Automatic traffic signal out
2 Automatic traffic signal partially defective
3 Permanent road signing defective or obscured
4 Road works present
5 Road surface defective

1.25 Carriageway Hazards

0 None
1 Dislodged vehicle load in carriageway
2 Other object in carriageway
3 Involvement with previous accident
4 Dog in carriageway
5 Other animal or pedestrian in carriageway

1.27 DOT Special Projects

56

Vehicle Record

2.1 Record Type
- 21 New vehicle record
- 25 Amended vehicle record

2.2 Police Force

2.3 Accident Ref No

2.4 Vehicle Ref No

2.5 Type of Vehicle
- 01 Pedal cycle
- 02 Moped
- 03 Motor scooter
- 04 Motor cycle
- 05 Combination
- 06 Invalid tricycle
- 07 Other three-
  wheeled car
- 08 Taxi
- 09 Car (four-wheeled)
- 10 Minibus / Motor caravan
- 11 Bus or coach
- 12 Light goods vehicle
- 13 Heavy goods vehicle
- 14 Other motor vehicle
- 15 Other non-motor vehicle

2.6 Towing and Articulation
- 0 No tow or articulation
- 1 Articulated vehicle
- 2 Double or multiple trailer
- 3 Caravan
- 4 Single trailer
- 5 Other tow

2.7 Manoeuvres
- 01 Reversing
- 02 Parked
- 03 Waiting to go ahead but held up
- 04 Stopping
- 05 Starting
- 06 U turn
- 07 Turning left
- 08 Waiting to turn left
- 09 Turning right
- 10 Waiting to turn right
- 11 Changing lane to left
- 12 Changing lane to right
- 13 Overtaking moving vehicle on its offside
- 14 Overtaking stationary vehicle on its offside
- 15 Overtaking on nearside
- 16 Going ahead left hand bend
- 17 Going ahead right hand bend
- 18 Going ahead other

2.8 Vehicle Movement Compass Point
From ☐ To ☐

Parked:
- not at kerb [0] [#]
- at kerb [*] [#]
  * code 1 - 8

- 1 N
- 2 NE
- 3 E
- 4 SE
- 5 S
- 6 SW
- 7 W
- 8 NW

2.9 Vehicle Location at Time of Accident
- 01 Leaving the main road
- 02 Entering the main road
- 03 On the main road
- 04 On the minor road
- 05 On service road
- 06 On lay-by or hard shoulder
- 07 Entering lay-by or hard shoulder
- 08 Leaving lay-by or hard shoulder
- 09 On cycleway
- 10 Not on carriageway

2.10 Junction Location of Vehicle at First Impact
- 0 Not at junction (or within 20 metres)
- 1 Vehicle approaching junction or parked at junction approach
- 2 Vehicle in middle of junction
- 3 Vehicle cleared junction or parked at junction exit
- 4 Did not impact

2.11 Skidding and Overturning
- 0 No skidding, jack-knifing or overturning
- 1 Skidded
- 2 Skidded and overturned
- 3 Jack-knifed
- 4 Jack-knifed and overturned
- 5 Overturned

2.12 Hit Object in Carriageway
- 00 None
- 01 Previous accident
- 02 Road works
- 03 Parked vehicle - lit
- 04 Parked vehicle - unlit
- 05 Bridge - roof
- 06 Bridge - side
- 07 Bollard / Refuge
- 08 Open door of vehicle
- 09 Central island of roundabout
- 10 Kerb
- 11 Other object

2.13 Vehicle Leaving Carriageway
- 0 Did not leave carriageway
- 1 Left carriageway nearside
- 2 Left carriageway nearside and rebounded
- 3 Left carriageway straight ahead at junction
- 4 Left carriageway offside onto central reservation
- 5 Left carriageway offside onto central reservation and rebounded
- 6 Left carriageway offside and crossed central reservation
- 7 Left carriageway offside
- 8 Left carriageway offside and rebounded

2.14 Hit Object Off Carriageway
- 00 None
- 01 Road sign / Traffic signal
- 02 Lamp post
- 03 Telegraph pole / Electricity pole
- 04 Tree
- 05 Bus stop / Bus shelter
- 06 Central crash barrier
- 07 Nearside or offside crash barrier
- 08 Submerged in water (completely)
- 09 Entered ditch
- 10 Other permanent object

2.16 First Point of Impact
- 0 Did not impact
- 1 Front
- 2 Back
- 3 Offside
- 4 Nearside

2.17 Other Vehicle Hit
Ref no of other vehicle

2.18 Part(s) Damaged
- 0 None
- 1 Front
- 2 Back
- 3 Offside
- 4 Nearside
- 5 Roof
- 6 Underside
- 7 All four sides

2.21 Sex of Driver
- 1 Male
- 2 Female
- 3 Not traced

2.22 Age of Driver
Estimated if necessary ☐ Years

2.23 Breath Test
- 0 Not applicable
- 1 Positive
- 2 Negative
- 3 Not requested
- 4 Failed to provide
- 5 Driver not contacted at time

2.24 Hit and Run
- 0 Other
- 1 Hit and Run
- 2 Non-stop, vehicle not hit

2.25 DOT Special Projects

2.26 Vehicle Registration Mark (VRM)
VRM or one of the following codes
- 2 Foreign / Diplomatic
- 3 Military
- 4 Trade plates
- 9 Unknown

57

Casualty Record

3.1 Record Type □□ `#`

- 31 New casualty record
- 35 Amended casualty record

3.2 Police Force □□

3.3 Accident Ref No □□□□□□□

3.4 Vehicle Ref No □□□

3.5 Casualty Ref No □□□

3.6 Casualty Class □

- 1 Driver or rider
- 2 Vehicle or pillion passenger
- 3 Pedestrian

3.7 Sex of Casualty □

- 1 Male
- 2 Female

3.8 Age of Casualty □□ Years

Estimated if necessary

3.9 Severity of Casualty □

- 1 Fatal
- 2 Serious
- 3 Slight

3.10 Pedestrian Location □□

- 00 Not a pedestrian
- 01 In carriageway, crossing on pedestrian crossing
- 02 In carriageway, crossing within zig-zag lines at crossing approach
- 03 In carriageway, crossing within zig-zag lines at crossing exit
- 04 In carriageway, crossing elsewhere within 50 metres of pedestrian crossing
- 05 In carriageway, crossing elsewhere
- 06 On footway or verge
- 07 On refuge, central island or central reservation
- 08 In centre of carriageway, not on refuge, central island or central reservation
- 09 In carriageway, not crossing
- 10 Unknown or other

3.11 Pedestrian Movement □

- 0 Not a pedestrian
- 1 Crossing from driver's nearside
- 2 Crossing from driver's nearside - masked by parked or stationary vehicle
- 3 Crossing from driver's offside
- 4 Crossing from driver's offside - masked by parked or stationary vehicle
- 5 In carriageway, stationary - not crossing (standing or playing)
- 6 In carriageway, stationary - not crossing (standing or playing), masked by parked or stationary vehicle
- 7 Walking along in carriageway - facing traffic
- 8 Walking along in carriageway - back to traffic
- 9 Unknown or other

3.12 Pedestrian Direction □□

Compass point bound

- 1 N
- 2 NE
- 3 E
- 4 SE
- 5 S
- 6 SW
- 7 W
- 8 NW
- 0 Standing still

3.13 School Pupil Casualty □

- 1 School pupil on journey to or from school
- 0 Other

3.15 Car Passenger □

- 0 Not a car passenger
- 1 Front seat car passenger
- 2 Rear seat car passenger

3.16 Bus or Coach Passenger □

- 0 Not a bus or coach passenger
- 1 Boarding
- 2 Alighting
- 3 Standing passenger
- 4 Seated passenger

3.17 DOT Special Projects □□□

Printed in the United Kingdom for The Stationery Office
J33358 C6 12/97 9385